GEOFF THOMPSON

Everything that Happens to Me is Good

summersdale

EVERYTHING THAT HAPPENS TO ME IS GOOD

Summersdale Publishers Ltd
46 West Street
Chichester
West Sussex
PO19 1RP
UK

www.summersdale.com

Printed and bound in Great Britain

ISBN: 1-84024-597-2
ISBN 13: 978-1-84024-597-4

As always, with big love and thanks to my beautiful wife Sharon for carrying my bones over some tough terrain.

Thank you to my lovely friend Margaret Ring for being an inspiration to me and my children over many a McDonald's coffee.

Also by Geoff Thompson

Contents

Foreword

Although I am primarily a writer of books and films, over the years I have also penned a bevy of articles for newspapers, magazines and my website. After many requests from readers (and several prompts from Richard Barnes, my friend and web master) I have decided to collect my favourites into the book you have before you now. I've also added a few extended and revised extracts from my book *The Elephant and the Twig* because they fit the ethos of this work. I personally love an uplifting article on the commute to work or a cerebral snack over lunch. (And whatever you do, don't give me a book to read in the loo – I might never come out again.)

There is something very satisfying and enjoyable (I think) about filling one of life's many stolen or idle moments with a good, quick read.

I hope this proves to be just that.

Geoff Thompson

Chapter 1

Be Nice

I read a fabulous poem once that has always stuck with me, not because it is sweet, rather because it is true. The poem went, 'I knew a man they called him mad the more he gave the more he had.'

I think we can assume from this small ditty that the man in question was a nice man who had stumbled upon one of life's great secrets: What you give out will return.

There is a massive profit in being nice, as long as you are not being nice for profit. And yet the mention of the reciprocality of genuine niceness does not seem to find its way into the reams of written work on doing business.

How bizarre.

In my pursuit of freedom through information I have studied everything from religion to spirituality, from theology to philosophy and law, and of course I have read – looking for inspiration – plenty about business; the art of making a living. I have read books by the guys and gals that have made it, lost it, lost it and made it back again, made it and given it all away, made it and squandered it, and even those that made it and hid the proceeds under the bed in a biscuit tin for fear of losing it all. The books have all been enlightening. Even the ones that were terrible taught me about where I didn't want to be. Many of the books talked about the win-win mentality, about ethics, about morals, about profit and loss, courage in business, risk taking, innovation, speculation, and dedication. Some quoted great sages, philosophers and gurus and taught about the dangers of money and power. But none advised me about the most important lesson in business: Be nice. Simply be nice. It is not hard. It costs nothing and it goes a hell of a long way (and comes back laden with profit).

The business world can often be a very difficult, cynical environment. People are often guilty of believing that everyone has an agenda – especially those who dare to be nice, those that dare to give and ask nothing in return. Those who scratch backs without asking for their own to be scratched are often judged with the utmost scepticism. Nobody does anything for nothing. There is no such thing as a free lunch.

But of course this is not true. The best, most attractive, most inspiring people in my world are all nice. They all do things for me – and for many others – with no thought of profit. They are all generous. They are all kind and do good deeds purely for the love of doing them.

What you give out always returns. Always. It is the law.

I have a friend, Paul Abbot, who is an incredibly successful writer. For those who don't know him, he is probably the top British TV writer of all time. He is responsible for (most recently) *Shameless*, *Clocking Off*, *State of Play*, *Touching Evil* and *Linda Green* to name just a few of the shows he's created. He is also an extremely generous man, both with his time and his advice. He has deals and contracts and commissions coming out of his very eyes. People are throwing work at him. His work is amazing; his work ethic even more so. You might think that his success is simply because of his hard work. You'd be wrong. If you go to his house and watch how he works you will see why he is so successful. He never stops being nice. He never stops giving. His house is like Euston Station on a Friday afternoon with all the comings and goings of the people he is helping. He is a dynamo. His capacity to help others to fulfil their own ambitions and dreams seems limitless. He gets in loads and loads of work and gives much of it away to new writers, struggling writers, often writers that the system has chewed up and spat out. And the more he gives away the more he seems to get back.

Similarly, I am always hearing stories about how nice my friend Glenn Smith is, and how many people he helps without asking anything in return. And my Auntie May (sadly now deceased) literally filled the room with her capacity to be nice and to give for no other profit than the joy it brought her. The great thing about Paul and Glenn and May is that most of the people they look after are not even in a position to return the favour, or offer them anything other than gratitude. And yet the more they give the more they seem to get. The effect is amazing. Glenn is thriving in business and life, as is Paul, and although my Auntie May is no longer on this plane, she has found immortality in the minds of many people (not least mine) just because she was so generous and nice.

Ultimately, I have found that people want to work with people who are nice. Even if – at this present moment in time – their game is not as sharp as it might be. If they are nice, people will help them tighten their game, people will go out of their way to find, even create work for them. People will bend themselves into all sorts of contorted shapes (including over backwards) so that they can help. And I am not talking about pseudo-nice, nice for the effect, nice to fit in or even nice to impress. If the nice you are offering is not of the genuine variety then it is a lie. Dishonesty in business is always the eventual harbinger of doom. I am only talking about the genuine article. Being nice because it helps others.

There is no profit in being nice, unless being nice is congruent with who you actually are. I am sure that to some of the hard-line business people out there this might sound a little trite: 'Be a nice person. People like it when you are nice.' I have even been told that there is no room in business for nice people. (Business types often mistake nice for weak.) But I would argue that if you are not nice, there will ultimately be no room in business for you.

The meek (as they say) will inherit the earth, and whilst profit may sojourn with those who do not heed the rules, it will only find permanent abode with those who do.

Chapter 2

Carp Fishing

I can remember (as though it were yesterday) a troubling internal conflict that I was wrestling with about five-years ago. I was teaching in the beautiful city of Edinburgh, Scotland with my friend Peter Consterdine. But teaching was just one of the myriad balls I was juggling at the time. I was also right in the middle of a very big book signing tour (for *Watch My Back*) that saw me visiting 60 shops in about 32 cities, of which Edinburgh was but one. As well as the tour, the teaching, and the heavy travelling schedule, I had also undertaken a huge financial risk when I decided to amalgamate all my bouncer books (*Watch My Back*, *Bouncer* and *On The Door*) into a hardcover omnibus edition and self-publish it in a bid to make *The Sunday Times* bestseller list. As you can imagine

14

I was stretched. But I was handling it OK, that is, until fate intervened. Someone – disgruntled by my work, my success, my profile, by me – decided to make it their life's mission to slander and threaten me via the Letters page of the very magazine I was a columnist in. Now you might think that this is par for the course when you are a profiled author, but with everything I was already carrying this one thing seemed to tip me over the edge. I was becoming anxious and angry. The nature of the letters – very personal and derogatory – were both unjustified and unfair, but they nevertheless found page space and were read by thousands. The publication of these letters actually made me question whether I really wanted to write for this magazine anymore. It made me question whether I wanted the profile I was receiving and, in fact, whether I wanted to actually be on the martial-arts scene at all if it spawned and seemingly encouraged such inane negativity. At any other time I probably would have left the slander where it belonged – in the bin. But with my mind stretched and vulnerable it found its way through my bullshit detector and was stabbing at my sensitive underbelly. I was troubled so I spoke with Peter about it one night in the bar of the Malmaison Hotel.

Peter has always been a mentor to me. In fact, he was the one who initially took me under his wing and helped me develop some very raw ideas into books, tapes and seminars. He is largely responsible for the success I enjoy in the martial arts today. Peter listened intently, nodded wisely (as he does) and said, 'Geoff, it's carp fishing!'

I said (more than a little confused), 'Carp fishing?'

Peter explained.

He told me that he was watching television one day and happened to catch a news story about a professional angler who appeared on TV regularly and had won a lot of major championships. He'd been riding the high-tide of success when something happened that changed, nay ruined, his life.

Just before one of the major championships, he was accused of using illegal bait. Now Peter didn't say whether our man was guilty or innocent, but what he did say was that the guy became so worried/angry/incensed and stressed about the accusation that he became depressed, started taking medication, split up with his wife and even lost his home. Peter told me how he'd watched the story unfold on television and, dumfounded, thought to himself, 'It's just carp fishing. It's not cancer, it's not war in the Middle East, it's not starving children in Africa. It's carp fishing.' This guy had become so engrossed in his sport that, what had started out as a gentle pastime, had actually become his whole world, it had become everything. It was more important to him than his wife, his family, his home. Apparently it had become more important that his health and his sanity.

What Peter pointed out to me, and what has stayed with me ever since, is the fact that the criticism I was receiving, far from being important, was just carp fishing. It was an opinion. And an opinion from some yokel who had never stepped into the arena himself, someone who was probably very angry because I was out there doing it, an individual, while he was one of the faceless multitude that liked to jeer from the bleachers because they were too scared to step into the ring. As Peter said to me, 'It's one man, Geoff, and a few letters. It's not life and death.'

This reminded me of another friend who went to see his father – a war veteran – for advise about a problem he was having. His father asked him, 'Is someone going to kill you?' My friend said no. His father said, 'Then you don't really have a problem.'

What I learned from this valuable lesson is that we often take ourselves and our problems way too seriously. We focus on them so intently that we lose our valuable sense of perspective, and when this happens molehills quickly start becoming mountains, and as we should all know, mountains can often be (or appear to be) insurmountable.

I suppose what I am trying to say is that it's all about perspective, about not letting things become bigger than they really are. It is very difficult for the eyes to see clearly what the mind has got completely out of focus.

Chapter 3

Catching Crabs

I watched a documentary when I was younger about how fishermen catch crabs (no, not them kind). I watched in awe as these leathery-faced, salty men of the sea lowered a mesh basket onto the ocean bed and, in no time at all, caught a couple of unlikely crabs that crawled in via a small hole in the lid and made their first (inadvertent) steps from basket to crabstick. What fascinated me most was not that they had crawled into what seemed an obvious trap; rather I was disturbed by the fact that they did not crawl back out again, even when the fishermen removed the lid. Eventually the basket filled to the brim with crustaceans, yet still they didn't try to escape.

After a few minutes it became clear to me why.

Every time a crab tried to crawl out of the trap, the other crabs (the blighters) pulled him back in again. I was amazed! I was watching my life's metaphor. Every time I had ever tried to leave a bad job and break away, my peers, like the crabs, had pulled me back again. 'What do you want to leave for?' they would ask patronisingly. 'This is a steady job. It's safe.' Then came the *coup de grâce*: 'There's no security out there, you know!'

'But I hate it here,' I'd whine.

'You haven't given it a chance! You've only been here five minutes,' came the usual response. (In fact, I'd been there six years.)

'So how long have *you* been here then?' I asked one day, tired of the unchanging replies. The old guy, face like a walnut, thought for a second. 'Oh about thirty years.'

'And what do you think of it?'

'It's crap,' he said without hesitation. 'I hate the place.'

Similarly, when I told my (ex) wife that I wanted to leave my steady job at the chemical factory, her face turned rolled-in-flour white. The old crab, claws raised, on the offensive, went straight to work.

'But what will we do? What if we don't make the mortgage? What if it doesn't work out? What if… '

It usually only took a few 'what if's' to get my blood boiling.

As I watched the documentary, I noticed that, after being pulled back a few times, the disheartened crabs not only stopped trying to escape but they also joined the other crabs in pulling back those that did try.

I'd been pulled back so many times in my life that I too felt disheartened. Self-depreciation became part of my inner core. The moment an entrepreneurial thought entered my mind, it was drowned by the voices of my inner crabs. Many times I picked up my biro in a fit of inspiration to write my way out of the factory by penning (what I dreamed would be) the next bestseller, only to be thwarted by a faulty internal dialogue that was stronger than my will to continue. So the pen would be discarded and replaced by bicycle clips and a ride to the factory for a night shift that I abhorred.

Even today, 20-years on, the very thought of that long ride still inspires a depression that reminds me how grateful I am to have found a way out. I used to sit in the works canteen in the dead of night when everyone else was tucked up in bed and think, 'What can I do to get out of this nightmare?' I felt so trapped. I had a family, a mortgage, HP payments, three children, a cat and a Raleigh Racer; so many things that kept me glued to a job I hated. And the longer I stayed the more glue I got stuck in. I could never think of anything else I wanted to do other than write, but I had allowed others to convince me that

I was dreaming and that this was not a real option.
I resigned myself to a nine-to-five, Monday-to-Friday
life of oil and grime.

But, I convinced myself, it wasn't my fault. I was stuck
in the factory because my wife wouldn't let me leave.

Then one night, after my usual session of
Sunday-evening bitching, my wife did something
unprecedented. She retracted her claws, told me to
shut my moaning gob and get a job that I did like if I
was so unhappy. She gave me her permission. Well, I
nearly fell over with the shock.

That was when the realisation hit me like a hefty tax
bill. She wasn't holding me back at all. My nightmarish
employment was no more her fault than it was the
fault of the old timers at the factory or my peers. The
fault was entirely mine. I was up to my kneecaps in
the brown stuff out of choice. Blaming others was
my way of hiding from my own fear. Those around
me only stopped me from climbing out of the basket
because I let them. I realised at this point – looking
in the mirror not at a hard-done-by 20-something
but at a frightened youth – that if I didn't want to
stay in a job, if I really wanted to leave the factory,
leave the city, even leave the country for that matter,
nothing and no one would be able to stop me. If I put
my heart and soul into doing something, believed it
could be done and had a little faith in my own power,
even mountains would crumble.

I could do anything, I could be anything. This was my world, my incarnation. I snatched back my free will.

Shortly after the shock of this realisation, I left my steady job of seven years and entered the real world of opportunity and excitement. I have never looked back. It was brilliant, exciting and scary. So much to do, so many places to go. I made a decision; I climbed out of the basket.

A few years later my mates were all made redundant from the secure 'job-for-life' in the factory. Me, I realised that the only security I needed was the knowledge that no matter what happened, I could and would handle it.

Chapter 4

Change Chaser

Have you ever heard the saying (and thought, 'What the hell does that mean?'): 'Be careful what you wish for because you might just get it.' I heard this saying many years ago and sort of innately knew what it meant, even if, at the time, I could neither articulate it nor act upon it.

To me, it meant that you should be careful when practising manifestation (the art of manifesting your desires and intentions) because it is an awesomely potent force that works. You will get what you steadfastly wish for, but getting what you want comes with a price tag. That price tag is change.

I have been thinking a lot of late about why people don't succeed in life, and why so many settle for second best when the whole world is open to them. I realised that the main reason for failure is not fear of failure but rather fear of success. I have witnessed so many people stand at the doorway to greatness only to balk and pull back at the last minute because, on looking through, they realised that success was not just a change of job title or an award or more zeroes in the bank, rather success was and is (often) a complete change of identity, a complete change of who you are. This change can cause temporary, even permanent disorientation.

Change is a word often bandied about with a flippancy that does not convey its potential for danger.

Only very few people in society really get this. Fewer still have the bottle to take on this danger, go out and, rather than run from the change, face it and chase it.

Change chasers are the leaders of this world.

Change is the one thing that we as a species tend to fear the most. Why do we fear this seemingly insignificant word? Because 'change' translated means death. Death of the old, the out-worn, the worn-out and the redundant. Gandhi had a radical suggestion regarding change. He said that we should, 'Be the change we want to see.'

In other words, we should not just sit and wait for the clammy grip of inevitability, we should not cower in a hole hoping that somehow change might pass us by on its perpetual sweep of the universe. It suggests that we should put in our gum shields, bang on our bag gloves, get into the fray and out of the spectator stands, take on the odds and challenge change to take its best shot. We should anticipate change and be on its crest as the great wave comes in, ride it and use its latent and innate power to drive us.

If you be the change you want to see you take away its sting, you de-fang it. If you can be the change, if you are the change, if you live the change, how can you fear the change? How can you fear what you are?

It is not change that hurts, only our resistance to it.

The good news is that whilst change might mean death, it just as certainly means birth. You can't have one without the other. They are the opposite sides of the same coin. Death of the old, birth of the new. When the caterpillar emerges from its chrysalis, we see the birth of the butterfly. It has to die to the old before it can be born to the new. Change is going to happen anyway whether you like it or not. It is the only constant. So you have a choice; to cower and hide from the inevitable or to be brave and *be* the inevitable.

There is as much freedom in acceptance of change as there is pain in resisting change. But our free will, God's great gift to mankind, offers us a choice, an exciting and empowering third option; to garner our courage and *be* the constant, *be* the change.

Have a look at your life right now. What changes are you hiding from? Which fears are pinning you down? What would you really love to do but at the same time fear to do?

Why not empower yourself today and turn the tables on change by stepping out to meet it? You might be surprised to find a brand-new shiny you just waiting to shapeshift and emerge.

Chapter 5

Easy

Amongst other things, I write films for a living. It's easy. It must be because it is all I hear people say these days. 'Geoff doesn't do a real job,' they say, 'he writes all day. Writing is easy.'

Really?

Writing is my passion. I love it. It is what I do. But easy? I don't think so. Perhaps it seems easy from the sidelines but then everything is easy from the spectator's stand. Perhaps for the ignorant and the inexperienced it seems easy, but then everything is easy in hypothesis. I have found that those who have yet to live up to their own standards will employ any available excuse to keep their pen and paper in different rooms rather than write the blockbuster they keep threatening to produce.

When I was ignorant and inexperienced I did and said exactly the same.

Let me give you an example of how easy my job is. This is important. If people keep thinking that success (in any field) is easy, they will be ill-prepared when reality smacks them between the eyes with demands for a steel fixer's work ethic, a saint's patience and the tenacity of a Titan.

My first film went into production in January 2007. People said, 'It happened so quickly. Overnight!'

So far I have been on this film for 12 years.

I have lost count of the amount of drafts I've written. Some of the early critique bordered on abusive. Every major film company in Britain turned it down several times. (One of my films has been turned down by 75 different financers. In this industry that is not unusual.)

When I wrote my book *Watch My Back* it was a similar story. Everyone said, 'Who wants to read a book about a Coventry bouncer? Leave your number in the bin.' It was turned down by more companies than I care to remember. If Sharon hadn't insisted I keep trying, I fear I might have taken the advice that I kept getting and thrown it in the bin. It hurt, of course, and the only way I stayed afloat was to use that criticism to give me drive. (I'll fucking show you.) It was that attitude that helped me get the book onto *The Sunday Times* bestseller list. It helped me write a stage play that had a national tour. It helped me write a short film that attracted international film stars, a BAFTA and entry into over thirty international festivals.

The film that won the BAFTA, *Brown Paper Bag* did not attract any financing at all. No one wanted to make it. It was too bleak, too harsh, had been done before. No one thought it was good enough to finance, so we (the producer, Natasha Carlish, who re-mortgaged her house for the film, and I) financed it ourselves. The many rebuttals tempered and energised me. Then I wrote a feature film and raised (with Martin Carr, the producer and Neil Thompson, the director) over two million pounds in finance. It is difficult when you feel that you are not getting any encouragement, of course, but... I liked it. I loved it. I developed an iron resolve. It weathered me like an old oak. All the rebuttals, knock-backs and criticism have helped me to develop a sinewy self-belief and a self-reliance that is so muscular it has its own respiratory system.

I could go on but I think the point it clear. No one has it easy. Life is difficult. But difficult is a necessary pre-requisite to success.

Chapter 6

Everest

A friend wrote to me. He was in bits. He'd applied for money from a local screen agency to produce a film he had written and they had returned his script with a rebuttal and a list of notes on how unprepared they thought he and his work were. The critique (he felt) was so scathing that it made his eyes water. I knew the feeling.

I have been there so often that I've actually developed bark over my exterior to help weather the critical storms. My friend had taken the critique (or the 'beasting,' as he saw it) all rather personally and was struggling to carry on. He told me that he was going to give up writing because the film world was (in his words) 'biased, behind the times, judgmental and a bastard to boot.'

This knock-back, one of many I presume (in this very subjective and very demanding business, rebuttal comes with the everyday post), had all but floored him. He felt his work was ready, in shape and filmable, but when the experienced industry folks advised him that it wasn't (not yet), he chose to see it as personal insult rather than qualified critique.

I tried to advise him that what he was experiencing was film-making (certainly it was a big part of the process) and that he should get used to it, because it is unlikely to get easier as you climb higher. It can be soul destroying, sometimes it's boot-in-the-bollocks painful, but you can't by-pass it.

With a slight change in perception, chunks of hardship can be moulded into the building blocks of strong character. Adversity and advance are synonymous and, after all, it was the north wind that made the Vikings.

My friend was attempting to ascend the Everest that is making a movie but struggling (and bitching about – please don't bitch about) the altitude. It is tough at the high end of any business, not least film-making, where millions are lost on bad films, and bad films seem to be more the norm than the exception. His email reminded me of a documentary I'd watched on TV and I told him about it in the hopes that it might inspire him to carry on, despite his set-back.

The film was about a super-fit man who wanted to climb Everest. To make his dream a reality, he trained his body to perfection until he was all sinew and muscle. He thought that this would be enough. It wasn't until he actually found himself on the mountain, at base camp, that he realised his stamina fell short of the mark. His training was good, meticulous even; he could run a fast marathon, lift heavy weights and captain his body and mind through the most excruciating physical workouts.

What he hadn't prepared for (what you can't really prepare for) was the actuality of being (as the Everest stalwarts are fond of saying) 'on the mountain.' Because on the mountain the air is thin. Even helicopters fall out of the sky in these higher altitudes because the spinning blades can't find purchase. The lack of air makes breathing – even for the fittest athletes – difficult. And the higher you go (as in life) the thinner the air gets. This is why on the higher echelons of Everest (and of life) there are very few people.

Now, although this man had been told many times in his preparations that the air on Everest was thin and that it would make progress slow and breathing difficult, he never really heeded the council. Until, that is, on day one when his chest was as tight as a fat kid's school shirt and he couldn't catch his breath.

He complained to his companions, all experienced climbers, that he couldn't breathe properly and they duly advised him (and reminded him) that, when you are on the mountain, this is the norm.

'No,' he insisted, 'you don't understand. I'm a fit man. I am conditioned. I should be able to breathe easier.'

Patiently the message was reiterated. 'There is very little air on the mountain. The higher you go the less there is. The inability to be able to get your lungs full is normal.' Again, he complained. He was fit. Not being able to breathe was not normal for him.

As much as his companions tried to reassure him that the way he was feeling 'was normal' (one climber said, 'Look, if you wake up in the morning feeling shit when you're on the mountain, it's a good day'), the neophyte climber would not have any of it.

He was convinced that his breathlessness was an early sign of some mysterious mountain illness. He bitched so much that in the end one of the climbers pulled him to one side and said (very firmly), 'Listen! We're on Everest. It's a high mountain. There is no air. If you want more air climb a smaller fucking mountain.'

And here endeth the lesson.

I need to hear it sometimes. I need to be told every now and then to 'stop the bitching and get on with it.' I am always trying to reach higher peaks and often find myself ready throw in the towel, complaining about the discomfort, the lack of help, the inadequate industry support. Then I remind myself of this story. It always gets me psyched up, back on my feet and moving. I don't know about you but I don't want to climb small mountains. I want to ascend into the clouds with the legends. And if that means less air (I haven't got much 'air anyway), then so be it.

Chapter 7

Everything that Happens to Me is Good

I heard it the other day and it made me smile, so much so that I went and made myself a cup of tea.

Someone said (with a hint of a scorn and a peppering of self-pity), 'That Geoff Thompson bloke, he lives a charmed life. He has had it so easy.'

Another friend, a fellow writer, tilted a similar lance in my direction. He told me that his lack of commercial success was due to the fact that he has had so many things block his path (poor health, family issues, etc.) I, on the other hand, had succeeded only because I'd had it so easy. He said this like nothing bad has ever happened to me; as though I was somehow impervious to the slings and arrows of life.

I have to come clean though. He was right. They were all right. I do live a charmed life and I have had it easy; not because nothing bad has ever happened to me, rather because everything that has happened to me has been good.

Let me try and explain.

My lovely dad died recently.

It was good.

It was his time and I was pleased that he finally got to graduate from this hard university we call life. It broke my heart to see him suffering so much whilst he was ill. I couldn't even talk on the phone without breaking down. He had cancer. It found its way into his bones. Then he died. My dad lived a good life. He was a good man. He was loved by many, disliked by none. But he has finished his brief sojourn on this spinning globe and now he is home. And that is not just good, it is cause for celebration. He has left me with a great legacy of love and very valuable lessons; how to live bravely, how to die with dignity.

One of my gorgeous babies took an overdose of pain killers when she was 18 years old. I got the five a.m. phone call and my heavy heart bled. A five-minute journey to the hospital took a lifetime and when I arrived all the doctors could tell me was, 'We won't know until tomorrow.'

It was a long day. It was an even longer night.

Someone said, 'Terrible what's happened to your daughter.' I said, 'What's happened to my daughter is the best thing that could have happened.'

My girl had fallen into a dark and loveless chasm where even the voices of her kin could not be heard. She was in a relationship that was imprisoning and dangerously destructive and none of us – not me, not her sisters, not her mum – could break her out. When she lay in that hospital bed, a small voice (somewhere in my consciousness) said to me, 'We are sorry she is here but this is the only way we could get her out.'

I trusted that this was true and it was.

She recovered, she went to university and met a nice guy who was appreciative of her beauty and sensitive nature. She is now happy and training to be a teacher. What happened to my daughter saddened me beyond words, but what happened to my daughter was good.

My brother died violently. He was bloated and yellow and ravaged and... so very beautiful. I have never felt such profound love for anyone as I felt for Ray during his five fast days of slow dying. I loved his very bones. But my brother loved the drink and the drink loved my brother, so much so that the love affair killed him. There was more to it than that, of course. Drink was his armoury and life was his enemy and, well, you can guess the rest. When he died, it was not me he called out for. It was not my mother's name that bounced and echoed off the hospital walls, nor my dad's, nor the names of any of his four heartbroken children. He cried out the name of his drinking companion, another alcoholic that shared his oblivious and sad existence. It was difficult. But it was good. The friend that passed the bottle in long days of hard drinking was very human and very broken and he loved my brother. For that reason alone, I loved him. I was with Ray as his decaying body buckled and bled and closed down. It was one of the most harrowing experiences of my life. It was also one of the most beautiful experiences of my life. I felt privileged that he chose me to watch his back as he left this life for the next. What happened to my beautiful brother has informed everything I do, everything I write about and everything I think. The lessons he taught me – both good and bad – I pass on. They will (they have and will again) save others.

My brother's death was good.

I have another family member who is dangerously ill. The illness is self-inflicted. My close family and I are forced to stand by and watch this slow decline because we can't save someone who will not be saved. It is her life. It is her body. It is her soul. It is her story. What is happening obviously needs to happen. It is her journey and it is good because all journeys lead home. That is ultimately where we are all heading.

I also have my own story. Much of it does not make easy reading, especially my back-story. I carry the karma of the hundreds of guys that I fucked up on nightclub doors when I worked as a bouncer. It has been hard to forgive myself. No self-pity here. No regrets. It was all good. The pre-fight, in-fight and post-fight have all been excruciatingly good. I am left with the residual ache of remorse, lessons that are as profound as they are stark and reference points that add an empirical wisdom to every new situation that I bring upon myself. Re-living each teeth-smashing boot to the face, each concussive stamp and each spitting invective has been... uncomfortable. In my former incarnation as a man of lower consciousness, I also fucked around, lost my integrity, betrayed my ex-wife, stole, fenced stolen goods and hurt my kids with my thoughtless actions. You don't just do that shit and walk away without debt. The trail follows you until you find the courage to turn and face it and take the consequences. We all have to atone. My actions spawned ten years of karmic residue that have brought me sadness, self-hate, guilt, self-harm and illness. Each of these, however, represented a step on the ladder of consciousness that has delivered me to where I am now; a better, more beautiful place, physically, mentally and spiritually.

So it has all been good.

Very good.

The experiences that fell into the realms of excess have been especially good. The road of excess (as the poet William Blake said) leads to the palace of wisdom. Every excess I indulged produced a lesson so painful, so profound, so earth-moving that it permeated my whole consciousness.

Although I vow never to repeat these dark experiences, I know that life will continue to proffer some of its own. It does have a habit of providing the hammer, anvil and furnace to temper every blade. So, if in life's next instruction I find myself revisiting those shadowy places, I will do my very best to neither spin nor toil, neither will I complain because it will all be good.

Everything that happens to me is.

And when folks say, 'That Geoff Thompson bloke, he's got it so easy,' I will continue to smile. I will continue to drink my tea. Because I know they're right. I do.

Chapter 8

Forgiveness: the Healthy Option

Have you ever noticed that when you mention things of a spiritual nature, eyes start to roll and conversational exits are surreptitiously sought? Is it, do you think, because the idea of seeking something unseen is completely at odds with today's body-obsessed culture? Myself, I've always had a deep interest in the spiritual. Though, I admit, during my woolly mammoth period as a bouncer it was buried beneath the fear of looking like a twat in front of my mates. Thus if spirituality came into the conversation I followed the norm and patronisingly 'eye-rolled' with the rest of the sheep. Now that I am a little more self-assured I don't need the kind of conditional security that the 'norm' offers. Instead I look to developing a deep-rooted internal security that is as steadfast as it is empowering. Where I once toiled for shallow, surface mastery – hitting hard, lifting heavy weights, looking good, building muscle – I now labour from the inside out, pumping 'cerebral iron' to build a deep, sinewy mentality. One of the hardest lessons I learned en route was the capacity to forgive.

They say that forgiveness is good for the soul. It is the doctrinal mainstay of just about every religious icon – from the Nazarene right through to Mahatma Gandhi – who has ever walked the earth. And yet when we examine the world in which we live, when we closely examine our own lives, we see that there are many people preaching forgiveness, but very few actually putting it into practise.

We claim to love those close to us yet we can't forgive our brother for a ten-year-old error in judgement, or our sister for some wrong she inflicted upon us last year. We can't forgive the foreman for the way he treats us on the factory floor, nor our neighbour for a minor misdemeanour. And we definitely can't exonerate ex-lovers for using us as a spousal punch-bag. It appears that we can't even forgive ourselves for stupid mistakes made on our own journey through life.

Oh, sometimes we feign forgiveness with the anaemic proclamation, 'I'll forgive you, but I'll never forget!' Or the equally unconvincing, 'I'll never completely forgive you!' But you can no sooner 'partially' forgive than you can 'partially' fall out of a tree. You either do or you do not.

We also have a great tendency to rationalise our blame with inane remarks like, 'Yea, but you don't know what she did to me. I can't forgive her.' We even seem perversely proud of ourselves when we don't forgive, as though it were a great virtue.

It is not virtuous. There is no great feat of strength in carrying the carcass of a long-dead argument. Holding a grudge is easy. You can do it without even trying.

To forgive! Now then, that's a horse of a different colour. It takes strength, discipline and great understanding in order to forgive. I believe it is a great weakness of the human spirit that forgiveness is not more widely practised.

Our lack of forgiveness is killing us – literally. Our failure to pardon manifests a resentment that grows with the passing of time. It becomes an internal time bomb of bitterness triggered and perpetuated by every unforgiving gesture. This has a catastrophic effect upon our physiology. Every time the grudge is replayed like an old movie in our mind's eye it activates the release of stress hormones into the blood stream, a physiological fight-or-flight. Your contentious thought is registered by the mid-brain as a physical threat, a saber-toothed tiger, if you like. But – and here's where the problems start – because the unforgiving thought is not physical threat but simply a reminiscence, behavioural fight-or-flight is not activated. We do not, therefore, run or fight for our lives so all those redundant stress hormones lay dormant in our bodies, acting like a toxic bath for the soft internal muscles like the heart, lungs, intestines, bladder and bowel. Even brain cells are killed by rogue stress hormones. Add to this the fact that your immune system is greatly impaired by the stress response and can't, under those circumstances, adequately defend the body against infiltrating viral and cancerous cells, and you have a recipe for disaster, even death.

It is already estimated that the majority of all contemporary illness finds its roots in stress.

So every time you relive past upsets (because you can't put them to bed with a heavy dose of forgiveness), your body actually relives them too, as though for the very first time. This means that someone who insulted you ten-years ago, who you haven't forgiven, is still insulting you today – and you're letting them!

Logically, the best way to stop people from hurting you is to forgive them. This is what author Charles Handy would call 'proper selfishness.' This exercise is not so much a means of helping others (though this too can be healthy) as it is a means of helping yourself.

Once you forgive a person you stop carrying them.

In my younger days, working as a nightclub bouncer, I held many grudges, and for several years. Every time I thought about my past tormentors I could literally feel the stress hormones going to work. I didn't realise that I was on a downwards spiral to ill-health. I am ashamed to admit that I was very proud of my collection of grudges and perennially laid them out on the table like favoured collectibles. I often bragged to others that, 'I will never forgive,' and 'one day I might even seek revenge.'

When I finally realised what I was doing to myself, or more specifically, what I was letting others do to me, I instantly let go of the past and forgave those who I had been carrying for so long. I felt as light as the proverbial feather. I also felt empowered. Now I always make a point of forgiving people when they upset my apple cart. I even try to forgive proactively before they even do anything to upset me.

Many people feel that forgiveness is a weakness and this discourages them from any active practise. In my experience, forgiveness is the shield and sword of the gods. It is a great strength that should be nurtured in all people.

Like most things in life it is better to start small and build up. Forgiveness needs to be localised. Forgive the small things and gradually build up to the big ones. Start with yourself. We all have skeletons in our closets. What ever they are, forgive yourself and move on.

As far as health and fitness is concerned, forgiveness is cathartic; an internal cleansing that is an integral piece of the longevity jigsaw. So if you want to stay fit for life, start with a little forgiveness.

Chapter 9

Goals

People often talk about success, about 'making it' and 'getting to the top.' Whilst goals are good and dreams are the stuff of life, neither is likely to transcend reverie without a little more detail and conviction. People want success but they don't know what in. They want to 'make it' but struggle to define the vital 'it' part of the equation. I admire those that aim for the top, however, I always find myself asking, 'To the top of what?' Ill-defined or vague goals need to be crystallised and put in print if they stand any chance at all of making it from fiction to fact.

In a famous survey carried out in 1953 at Yale University, each and every student was asked their views on a number of topics relating to the university; what they thought of the campus, the staff, the library, and the lecturers. Even their opinions on the campus canteen were sought. Every imaginable question about life at Yale (and in fact, life itself) was posed. One of the most intriguing questions asked of the final-year students was, 'Do you have goals?' This question was followed by, 'If you have goals, do you write them down?' Only ten per cent of those surveyed actually had goals and of these only a minute four per cent said they actually wrote their goals down.

Interesting, you'll probably agree; even disappointing. But not enough to write home to mum about. What was interesting, even disturbing, was the follow-up survey some twenty years later when Yale repeated the exercise. This time, rather than pose the same set of questions to the current crop of final-year students, they decided to throw a bit of currency at the project and find all the people from the original survey of 1953 to see if their youthful aspirations had come to fruition.

It was agreed, and after much globetrotting research the majority of those surveyed twenty years before were found and asked, 'How did your life turn out?'

Amazingly, the four per cent who had written down their goals were all hugely successful, in their health, their relationships, in their community and financial affairs. They were outstandingly different from everyone else surveyed. The four per cent were also financially independent. In fact, between them

they were worth more than all the other 96 per cent
– those who did not write down their goals – put
together.

What this should tell you is that having life goals
is not just important, it is fundamental. If you don't
have them, you don't get them. And if you want them
badly enough you'll make that extra commitment to
write them down. It makes them official. You need
a definite destination. How can you ever get there if
you don't even know where 'there' is?

If you have ever read a motivational book you'll
probably know this already. The word 'goal' is
tumbling from the motivational lips of just about
every success guru from Deepak Chopra to Anthony
Robbins. And they are right. But what most sellers
of success fail to mention is the fact that success (in
whatever form you would like it) comes at a price.
And I am not necessarily talking about money, but
about time, risk, commitment and sacrifice. Goals
cost and for those of us unable or unwilling to pay,
fulfilment is rarely forthcoming. Rather than make
these sacrifices and actively seek out their dreams, the
majority sit waiting for success to come to them – and
for free. They wait for providence and fortune to show
them favour. But the millions seldom come to those
who do not develop the millionaire mentality. Income
and lifestyle rarely exceed personal development. So
if you have a goal what you have to ask yourself is:

Am I prepared to pay the price and become the type of person it will take to get my goal?

I look at my friend Glenn, for instance. He is in fabulous physical shape. He has the kind of rippling torso that most men dream of seeing reflected back at them in the bathroom mirror; lots of sinewy muscle and no fat (don't you just hate that?) He's ripped like a skinless chicken. But of all the people that come to the gym looking to achieve a similar body, probably only five per cent ever end up looking like Glenn. Why? Because the 95 per cent are not prepared to become the type of person they need to be to get a beach physique. They don't want to pay the price. To get 'cut-up from the gut-up' you need to chart the right course, then have the discipline and the staying power to stick to it without deviating to the island of cake, or the port of beer-and-curry. To build a body like Glenn you have to make sacrifices and develop a powerful will that'll resist the Friday-night piss-up/Saturday-morning fry-up scenario that follows a working week at the computer. You need to set a course from where you are to where you would like to be. And to show your commitment that goal needs to be written down and deadlined (time limits can be extended or shortened, if necessary).

Diet – the ultimate discipline – is the pre-requisite of a good physique. You have to get your eating down to a fine art. But very few make it because the journey is too arduous. Some kid themselves that they can take out the bits they don't like (usually diet) and still make their destination. Certainly the early stages are difficult when you have to change a 25-year-old cake-and-cookie habit and replace it with a high-protein/low-fat regime.

Next on the course is the training. I know a million people that workout, but I only know one or two with anything like a good shape. Whenever I go to the gym I see people sweating their way around the free-weights and machines, making all the right noises. But a hard workout is not just about the sweat and strain. It's about the detail, working on the finer points and setting the right course.

Setting the right course

It is easy to say, 'Set a course to where you want to go and you'll get there.' People set courses all the time and still fail to reach their goal. This is usually because they inadvertently set the wrong course and end up at the wrong destination, or even worse, back where they started. You might be working extremely hard but are you working in the right direction?

I remember the time I wanted to develop a brilliant osoto-gari (a throwing technique in judo). I'd watched good judo players perform the move a thousand times. I'd seen detailed illustrations in books and even watched demonstrations of the throw on instructional videos. With my limited knowledge I set about achieving my goal. I practised hard and daily. I have always prided myself on being a tenacious – even obsessive – trainer. I practised osoto-gari thousands of times, to destruction in fact, but I was practising it wrong. Never mistake activity for progress. You could be the hardest worker in the world, but still fail because you are hacking away in the wrong jungle.

The destination was set, but my course was off; it only has to be slightly out for you to end up completely wrong. I became brilliant at doing osoto-gari the wrong way. Consequently, when I sparred with other players, I rarely pulled the throw off. Then I went to train with Neil Adams (Olympic silver medallist in judo). He knew the right way to do osoto-gari. He knew the right course. He looked at my technique and, in altering one or two minor points, he altered my entire course. And hey, presto, I got it. In fact, because I had been given the right map and wanted to get there badly enough, I reached my goal in record time.

So make sure that you set the right course and be prepared for the sacrifices that the journey demands. If you don't know the way, ask the right people, those who are already where you want to be.

The danger of goals

Goals are essential; we've established this much. And writing the goal down with an expected time of arrival is as pivotal as setting the right course. But as well as all the obvious risks of aiming high – the risk of failure, risk of success and risk of change – there is also a hidden risk: Goals can be dangerous. When we set goals, when we fully intend with all our heart to achieve them, we nearly always do. So what's the danger in that? The danger occurs when we don't set our goals high enough.

Sometimes we aim low and, guess what, we hit low. Small goals are fine when they act as stepping-stones to higher ideals, but they can be very unsatisfactory in themselves.

My friend Steve is a keen runner. The other day he went out for a jog. He set himself a goal of five miles. He was capable of more, 'But,' he always told me, 'I'm being realistic. I know I can do five. If I try for more, I might not make it.' Not the sort of mind-set that smashes records, I think you'll agree, but a common attitude nevertheless. He set five miles on his internal clock and his body fuelled him up for exactly that. By four-and-a-half miles he was flagging and every step was an effort. He made five miles but at the final furlong the lad was exhausted.

The next week, Dave, one of his friends at the running club, had to pull out of a ten-mile race. He asked Steve to take his place. Steve was unsure. He didn't think he could run ten miles; it was double his usual distance.

'Don't worry,' Dave said, 'just set your sights on ten. If you can't finish it's not the end of the world.' Steve ran the race, killed the ten miles and had a great time doing it. He injected necessity and the organism grew to compensate. He is now preparing for his first marathon.

If you set your sights too low your body and mind will fuel you accordingly. Setting achievable goals does not push and stretch our limits; implementing standards that are just beyond our reach does. Paradoxically, I would say, 'Don't set your sights so high on the first shot that you become overwhelmed.' Had Steve gone from a five-mile jog to the London marathon (26 miles) he might well have written a cheque that the bank could not honour.

So aim higher than you think you can manage, but not so high you lose sight of your goal.

Milo the Great

There is a wonderful story about Milo the Great, a historical strong man whose life goal was to carry a full-grown bull on his shoulders.

'Impossible,' said his friends.

'Oh yea?' he replied. 'Watch this space.'

Milo was strong both mentally and physically, but he knew he was not burly enough to carry a full-grown bull. So instead of making his way to the nearest farmer's field and trying to winch a horned beast onto his back, he went out and bought himself a calf and kept it in his back garden. Every day Milo would go out into the yard and – after a little warm-up – lift the calf onto his shoulders and walk around with it. Day by day, as the calf matured and fattened, Milo's strength grew to compensate. His legs expanded in width and strength and his torso transformed into the shape of a door wedge. Eventually, Milo – to the astonishment of all – could carry the full-grown bull on his shoulders. By picking up the bull as it grew, and subsequently pyramiding his own strength to match, he grew with the bull.

Your bull may not be a hairy creature with horns and a nose-ring (sounds like a girl I once dated), rather it might be your business, a college degree or a promotion at work. Perhaps your goal is to buy your dream house (with a bull-sized mortgage). It could be anything. Like Milo, you don't have to pick up the bull right away. It isn't always advisable to try. Instead, you should allow your growth to be gradual and organic.

For Milo, picking up the bull was done in pyramidic stages. He used short-term goals (picking up the calf every day) to power him towards his long-term ideal. You could use the same principle to buy your dream house, build your business or increase your fitness level. Many people have bought fabulous homes by using the calf/bull principle. They buy a small house, sell it and use the profit (plus their savings, perhaps) to move up the property ladder towards their dream cottage in the country. It can be done. Hard work? No harder than working your doo-daas off with no goal in mind.

I'm not saying that this is the only way. You can jump steps, climb up more than one rung at a time, but when you do the risk rises proportionately. It's all down to how much risk you can take. Some people crumble when danger comes aboard. Others thrive on it.

Goal pyramid

You could even build a goal pyramid to chart your steps from short-term to long-term goals. Mountaineers do this to allow themselves recuperation and acclimatisation to new heights. They make their way first to a base camp, acclimatise, then step by step, they scale to the summit of the mountain. When they get within reach of the top they rest, eat, acclimatise and then, when the weather is clement, they attempt the peak. It is all done in pyramidic steps. They set themselves daily goals, aiming to climb x amount of metres by nightfall. If conditions are favourable, they may (and often do) exceed their quota; on bad days they may not even leave the tent.

I remember my mum using this principle to help my dad lose weight. He was carrying a belt-busting belly that was getting unhealthy (and unsightly) but he wouldn't hear of going on a diet. His self-discipline wasn't up to the job. My mum, worried about his health, gradually started to cut the size of his dinner down a tiny bit at a time and over a long period. Before he knew it he was eating light and healthy meals and looking and feeling good. As the dinner sizes decreased, the weight fell off him. It was so gradual he hardly noticed.

The real value of setting goals is not, as you might imagine, in their achievement – arriving at our destination is secondary. The greatest benefit of setting and achieving goals is the skills, the discipline, the tenacity, the information and the leadership qualities you'll develop along the way. Your whole world will change immeasurably for the better as a consequence. The adversity of a hard climb is what forges character.

Follow the Yellow Brick Road

In the film *The Wizard of Oz*, Dorothy and her troupe of mates are seeking a common ideal – the Wizard, a man who (they believe) can help them to achieve their individual goals. Dorothy wants to get back home to Kansas, the Cowardly Lion wants to find courage, the Tin Man needs a heart and the Scarecrow is desperate for a brain. Each of them believes that the Wizard will simply give them, free of charge, their dream. But he doesn't. He can't. What he can and does do is give them the means to achieve their dreams. He sends them on a hunt and promises to help them when they return. After accidentally killing the Wicked Witch of the West ('I'm melting, I'm melting') they return to Oz. The Wizard reluctantly keeps his word. He gives the Cowardly Lion a medal of valour, the Tin Man a heart-shaped watch, the Scarecrow a university diploma and Dorothy the knowledge that the power to return home was in her all along. Whilst each believes they have been given their goal free of charge, in actuality they have, through their journey – first to Oz and then to kill the witch – earned it through their own efforts. On the journey, the Cowardly Lion develops courage by facing his fears and protecting his friends against the witch and her army of mad, flying monkeys. The Scarecrow develops his brain by working out intricate game plans to find and then escape the witch. The Tin Man develops a heart through a multitude of kind and charitable acts. What the Wizard gives them amounts to little more than trinkets, symbols of their courageous quest. Their real goal started to manifest when they committed themselves fully to the task and agreed to pay the toll and take the risks.

Goals are as individual as fingerprints and one man's nirvana is often another man's nervous breakdown. Whatever your goal, there is one thing I have learned and one thing I know: We can achieve anything, nothing is beyond us. If we set our goals to paper and intend them to happen, mountains will move and rivers will part.

When I look at my lofty, long-term objective from the safety of my king-sized duvet, I don't ask myself, 'Can I have this goal' because I already know I can. I can have anything, we all can. Rather I ask myself, 'Can I become the kind of person it will take to get it?' Who we become is far more important than what we get.

Chapter 10

Gratitude: a Bit of Invisible Support

Sometimes we get so caught up in the maelstrom of life, ambition and achievement that we fail to realise what is really important in our lives; our health and the love and health of those dear to us. We forget to stop and thank God for all that we have, all that we have had and all that we will receive in the future. I know that I am often guilty of this and it is something that I intend to remedy because gratitude is more vital to our well-being than money or position or prospects. It is only after we hit a snag in life – an illness, a loss, depression – that we stop to appreciate just what we have. It often seems that we don't really appreciate our lot until it might be taken away from us.

When I look at the people I admire – Jesus Christ, Deepak Chopra, Gandhi and Mother Teresa – I notice that they all start their day with meditation and prayer. A big part of their daily ritual consists of thanking God for everything they have. They start their day not by asking for more, but by giving thanks for what they have already received and for what they know they will receive in the future. Not only does this morning mediation give them the chance to offer gratitude, but it also gives them the opportunity to fuel-up – spiritually, mentally and physically – for the day. This is how great people achieve great things.

Mother Teresa said that without her morning prayer and meditation (like Deepak Chopra she started early in the day, from four until six a.m.), she could never have sustained herself throughout the day. The spiritually aware are not in the habit of relying entirely upon themselves to achieve great things. They rely on God and through Him all things are possible. We all need a bit of invisible support, even – perhaps especially – when we think we don't. Great people don't get themselves in a muddle (too often) and then run to prayer (like most of us) to get fixed up. They pray preventatively so that they don't end up in a muddle in the first place. One ounce of prevention, after all, is better than a pound of cure. It's a bit like filling your car with fuel in the morning in anticipation of the day's journey. It would be unwise to just get up and drive your vehicle until it runs out of fuel. If you are lucky you may end up broken down only yards away from a nearby garage (not too much of an inconvenience). You might, however, end up broken down miles from anywhere with a long and inconvenient walk to the nearest fuel station.

I don't know of anyone who has not reached a crisis point at least once in their lives and thought, 'I'll get myself right and then I'll change (and I mean it this time).' And then they get themselves right and they change, but the change only lasts long enough to get them out of the rough and then 'bang!', they (me, you, all of us) end up falling back into their old ways and the pain of the past is hardly remembered. What I am suggesting here – and this is as much for me as it is for you – is that the change you are always threatening (better diet, being more patient, less jealous) is far better implemented from the solid clearing of the healthy here-and-now than it is from the out-of-balance, destined-to-arrive tomorrow. It takes discipline, insight, courage and a heck of a lot of self-knowledge. But if you were to start now, while the idea is fresh in your mind, then before you know it you would be riding the next wave rather than being bashed against the rocks (again).

They say that pain is a good advisor, and it is. But – as the saying intimates – it involves pain. Now if we were able to employ honest perception ('I know what needs to be changed') and a bit of will ('I am strong enough to make that change'), we could avoid the worst pain by tackling it while it is still just a niggle on the periphery of our knowing.

Or you could simply wait (like the last time) to get yourself buried up to the neck in problems and then try and muster the courage to pull yourself back out again, likely with the promise that, 'I'll get myself right then I'll change (and I mean it this time').

Chapter 11

Have Your Cake and Eat It

Go into any bookshop worth its salt and you'll find a pile of books and magazines offering the latest lose-fat-and-still-eat-chips diet that will allow you – or your money back – to have your cake and eat it. Now I don't know about you, but as a man with the propensity to grow, after a two-week holiday in Florida, to the size of a small continent, I have tried all the fad diets. And they all work... but only for a while.

Almost as soon as you lose the pounds (sometimes stones) and your jeans stop straining at the seams, the very same weight – and a bit more (for inflation, I presume) – returns with a vengeance and you have to make new holes in your belt.

It's depressing, isn't it?

It wouldn't be so bad but all the really tasty stuff simply oozes fat-gut, weight gain. I only have to look at the biscuit barrel and I grow another chin. As little as a week on a take-away fest leaves me with a skin-coloured bum-bag that wobbles in time with my step. I can be good for months at a time, sometimes even longer, and my weight stays at a comfortable 13 stone nine. The minute I get a fry-up down my neck, though, my legs start going all Sumo.

When I was 19 and clothes-line thin I could empty the contents of an industrial fridge without clocking up a single extra number on the bathroom scales. In fact, I was so thin that I wanted to put on weight, but my in-a-hurry metabolism burnt calories as quickly as I could extract them from Kit-Kats and kormas.

Then I hit 30.

At thirty my internal calorie-crunching gizmo switched to a lazy three-day week. All of a sudden the nuts and crisps, the beers and curries started to take their toll and I developed what can only be described as a wide-load arse. My food-abuse period was over; the salad and chicken renaissance lay in wait.

From then on in my weight has gone up and down like a busy lift.

When the weight is off I float around like a feather-light thing in tight fitting tee shirts tucked into bottom-hugging jeans, nibbling on health biscuits that taste like manila envelopes. I take every opportunity to remove my top and bare my torso, even when the wind is whistling my nipples into biker studs.

When I'm thin, my self-esteem rises to the rooftops.

When the weight is on, however, a dark cloud descends on my day. My world becomes one of chip dinners (I hide away in greasy-Joe cafes), rationalisation, take-away curries, wine, and beer and puddings that I might as well mould right onto my belly. And the apparel changes accordingly; beltless trousers with the top two buttons undone, hidden by trench-coat sweatshirts that obliterate everything from the neck to the knees. Even sex takes a backseat because it involves nakedness and hours of holding in my belly. My self-esteem drags around behind me like a wedding train.

As I said, I have tried them all; high-protein diets that turn your stools to rocks (ouch), high-fibre diets that have you shitting through the eye of a needle, low-carb diets that leave you so hungry you start nicking food off the kids' plates and snacking on carpet tiles, food-combining diets that are so complicated your brain throbs like a hammered thumb and sends you racing to the nearest chippy for a carb/fat/calorie top-up. A man needs his strength after all.

And the fruit diet! What's that all about then? I've been on it and no matter how hard I've tried I can't make a grape look or taste like a Malteser!

So what is the answer? How do I keep my sylph-like physique with all the culinary temptations constantly battling to fatten me up?

After 40 years of counting calories, hunting for the fat content on the backs of crisp packets and watching my bungee-belly bounce backwards and forwards from six pack to party seven, I've come to the conclusion that disciplined light eating for the rest of my life is the only way to stop me from looking like a doughnut. It's difficult, and you can never let up, but it works. Have some of what you want, but not all of what you want; train every other day and you'll keep the fat-monster at bay.

I dream that the Hereafter might be a paradoxical universe where Mars Bars and crisp sandwiches are the vital sustenance of life. In the meantime, I'm going to heed my mum's advice (offered to me when I hit a hefty 16 stone): 'Walk past that chip shop, Geoffrey.'

Chapter 12

Intention

There has been much written of late about intention. Some say (and I agree with them) that intentions are the building blocks of the universe. What you strongly intend today you are sure to live out in all your tomorrows.

This is both exciting and terrifying.

Most of us are not well-practised with our intentions so we tend to create our universe accidentally, complete with cloud-bathing heavens and barrel-scraping hells. When we are in heaven we call it a fluke or a happy accident. When we are in hell we call it 'karmic return' or we talk about 'spiteful God.' The truth is neither. We are creators of denial, fashioning random realities with our unskilled and unschooled thoughts, then looking outside ourselves to praise or blame when our creation makes us happy or sends us into a dizzy depression.

People with a lower level of consciousness revel in the blame culture. It is not their fault that life is shit so they look for someone, anyone, to blame. This is a weak place to reside because it is so disempowering. There is no darker place than the one you're in when you're playing the blame game. The very act of blaming gives your power over to the object of your blame. If you blame God, then it means your situation will not change until God favours you. Similarly, if you blame the government, society, your country, city or town, if you blame your ex-wife or mate or teacher, then you give them the key to your cell and await their leniency.

You always become a prisoner of those you blame.

People with higher levels of consciousness always place themselves at cause. They blame no one. They understand that their reality is one of their own making and if they want to change it they have only to look to the man or woman in the mirror. This gives them the freedom to practise their intentions until they become expert enough to create something dazzling.

Those who blame do so because (deep down) they are afraid of responsibility. It is easier to hunt down a culpable scapegoat than it is to take the blame onto your own shoulders. Those that take responsibility do so because they are excited about the possibilities of creating a new and ever-improved reality.

Personally, before I accepted responsibility, I resided consecutively, sometimes concurrently, in both worlds.

In my time I have created health, wealth, happiness and material possessions with my very best intentions, whilst at the same time creating violence, illness, unhappiness and penury with my very worst. It was only when I took a hard and honest inventory of my life that I realised I was the creator of it all. I could trace every good and every bad result back to intentions – or strong and persistent thoughts – that I'd had. It was at this point that I got very scared. And it was at this point that I got very excited.

I was scared because although I realised I'd created this juxtaposition of realities, I wasn't exactly sure how. That made my reality very unpredictable. I was excited because I knew I could learn by using my own inadvertent experience as a reference point. I could learn from my own experience. And where the details were foggy I could borrow from the library of information that is currently available on the power of intention. I could become an expert and I could practise as much as I wanted.

And that is what I did.

So how do you practise intention?

First you have to accept that intention is a creative force. Not just your own intention, but the universal intention that you click into when you practise. If you don't at least have an intellectual understanding of your own power then you are doomed to spin in an ever increasing cycle of random creation where life will bring you joy one day and a punch in the eye the next.

Search out the truth from another source, if you desire. It is in the Bible, it is in the Bhagavad-gita, the Koran, and the Tao Te Ching. Buddhism's basic tenant is that we create our own universe. Even new science is catching up with theories of Quantum mechanics (see the film, *What The Bleep Do We Know* or look at Deepak Chopra's work on the science of intention).

Once you accept the premise the training can begin.

You practise intention the same way as you would practice anything that you want to become expert in; with study and diligence. To become a strong judo player I read everything on judo. I placed myself in front of world-class teachers, I talked judo, I watched judo, I actually lived and breathed judo. But more than anything else I practised judo. I drilled and drilled and drilled the techniques until I was expert, until I could close my eyes and feel them, until I was the techniques and could handle judo players on the international scene.

Intention is no different. If you are a weekend player, you will get weekend results. If you practise four or five times a week, you'll start to see some decent movement. If you make it your life, you will rise rapidly into the higher echelons.

You start by investing in the information and instruction. Buy the books (my book, *The Elephant and the Twig*; any of Deepak Chopra's works; *The Field: The Quest for the Secret Force of the Universe* by Lynne McTaggart), attend the seminars (if you don't invest in you who will?), then practise what you have learned and be the proof that it works. There is nothing like actual hands-on experience to cement a truth in place.

For me, intention is about everything I do. If I want to create good health then I intend good health by seeing it, hearing it, reading it, talking it and doing all the things that constitute good health. If it is wealth I am after, then I do the same thing. I dwell on wealth until I start to draw it, or the opportunities to make it, into my life. People that make themselves ill practice intention without realising it. They think illness, they see and fear illness, they talk it, read it, watch it and live it until eventually they manifest all the fine and grizzly details in their own bodies.

I have a friend of a friend who is a very successful woman. She is at the top of her field. It wasn't always that way. When she was younger and her mind was undisciplined she was always suffering with psychosomatic illnesses that would often lay her up for weeks, sometimes months at a time. She even convinced herself once that she had a brain tumour. She thought about it all day long. She read about tumours in her medical books and read articles about the symptoms in medical journals until, in a short time, she actually started to manifest these symptoms herself. She became so convinced she had a brain tumour that she went blind in her left eye. She was finally taken into the hospital for a brain scan. The scan was clear. There was nothing physically wrong with her. She had no tumour. Interestingly, as soon as she got the results, the sight in her left eye returned. Then she had a thought; if her mind was so powerful that it could manifest blindness, how much more could she manifest if she schooled and disciplined her thought and put her intention to work on good things?

People that create great wealth click into the same power. When the actor Jim Carey was going through a very difficult phase as a stand-up comedian he drove up to Mulholland Drive in the Hollywood hills and decided that he was no longer prepared to work for peanuts. He was no longer prepared to be an also-ran stand-up comedian dying on stage night after night in front of a partisan crowd. So he took his bank book out and wrote himself a cheque for $10 million. He vowed that he would be earning that amount per film within ten years.

He was wrong.

Ten years later he was an actor in Hollywood, but he wasn't earning $10 million. He was earning $20 million. His intention was so solid that he wrote it down and then never lost the faith until his dream was a reality.

You practise by doing, and doing involves thinking, seeing, hearing, feeling, smelling and intuiting your intention until your thoughts coagulate and become manifest. Whether you intend to paint the front room or climb Mount Everest, the process is the same.

Intention is a very learnable technique. If you can learn to drive then you can learn to intend. And if you intend enough, you can become an authority.

Why not try?

Chapter 13

Looking Out, Looking In

Another marathon, another black belt, another gruelling, physically-stretching, pain-inducing endeavour where we venture out bravely to our furthest limits. The elements are conquered. We get a pat on the back, a medal, a trophy, admiration from our peers and awards stacked up on our shelves. How brave, how exciting, how very fucking invigorating. We take a little rest then onto the next extreme challenge, the next unchartered landscape that we can not only attack but also tell our friends that we are going to attack so that they can flatter us with their admiration. The praise comes at us like a sickly sweet chocolate waterfall and we let it shower over us.

It's good to be brave.

But how brave are we?

Do we choose the fights that we know we can win (even though we tell ourselves how extremely dangerous they are?) Are we guilty of racing out there pretending to look for the unchartered when actually we know that all of it is chartered and – although certainly physically demanding – has been done before?

In order to be really brave, to be really extreme, to be really daring and adventurous and to really (I mean really) look death in the eye and take our hearts (and our arses) in our hands, we need never do another climb, race another marathon, face another black belt panel or fight another monster on the nightclub door. In fact, I'd say that if we really want to stop pretending, we don't need to leave the city that we live in, the town, the road, the street, the house, the room or even our own skin, ever again. If we really want to be brave we just need to close our eyes, stop going out and start going in.

Fuck Nanga Parbat, fuck the one-hundred-man kumite, fuck the marathon across the desert or the triathlon across broken glass in bare feet. Fuck all of that because it is old hat, it has all been done. That old parrot of a challenge is dead. It is all boringly predictable compared to the real challenge of going inside and taking a cold, hard, honest look at yourself – and then changing the bits that no longer serve. Actually, even before that it would be a start to admit the fact that the man or woman that you look at in the bathroom mirror every day is deeply flawed. The man or woman with ten black-belt certificates in ten different styles from ten different masters who the outside world thinks is granite tough is not even tough enough to leave the job they hate, the spouse who treats them badly, the city that no longer nourishes them and the habits that bleed them dry because they are frightened of real change. Real change is full of uncertainty.

The man who impressed the living shit out of everyone by climbing ten peaks in ten months and who lost ten toes to frostbite is not even strong enough to resist temptation. Instead, he loses his integrity by sleeping with his best mate's wife. For a five second spurty tingle of cloudy liquid, he loses his soul.

Most of us think we are tough but most of us are not even tough enough to deal with the greed and envy in our gut, the panic and fear in our chest, the repressed rage that is hooked and fish-boned into the flesh of our throats or the jealousy that rages in our heads. We feel tough but we can't control what we eat and what we drink and what we ingest. We feel strong yet we let our thoughts kick sand in our faces. We feel manly and yet we fear to cry. We claim power and yet we lack even the power to change.

So we go out, we do courses, we listen to lectures, we take yoga (five different styles), we lift weights, or go to step class or learn Qui Gung or Tai Chi. We read the Bible, we devour the I-Ching or memorise the Bhagavad-gita. When we feel spiritual we quote Lao Tzu and when we feel angry we fire invectives from Sun Tzu. We talk about the Upanishads ('What, you haven't read the Upanishads?'), we meditate, contemplate, whirl like a dervish, chant, have homeopathy, get our feet massaged, have our scalps fingered by a dark-skinned chip fryer from Bolton, do the tarot, have our runes read, visit spiritual healers, sun worship, go on a fucking retreat and talk to fucking trees.

We go out and we do it all. And that's the point. We are going out but we're not going in. Out there is the path that is so well-travelled that the ground is flat. There is only one path that is not only less travelled, but not fucking travelled at all. That is that one true path that leads us into the murky quarry, the slushy cerebral dumping ground where the decomposing (but still very alive) bodies of our pasts lie waiting not only for their reckoning, not only for their release date, not only for their say but for their redemption.

It is hard to look at what you did, what was done to you, how you were treated and how you treated others. It is hard to look the many versions of the old you in the eye and say, 'Actually, I don't like you. I don't like what you are, what you did. I don't like what you didn't do. I don't like what you became.

I don't like what you allowed yourself to become. I don't understand you.' That's difficult. That's a mountain to climb, that is a fearsome one-hundred-man kumite (each opponent a version of the old you with a grudge to bear and a bloody axe to grind), but it gets even harder. To ensure the release of these trapped entities you don't just have to acknowledge them and look them in the eye; you have to face them and say, 'I forgive you, I forgive them. I let me (all of me) go. I let them go.'

Do the marathon if it serves you. Climb the mountain if it is a workout you are looking for. But if you really want peace, stop working out and start working in.

Chapter 14

Night-travellers

I thought you might be interested in a conversation I had at the weekend with my writer friend, Paul Abbot. Most of us spend our days looking for comfort and avoiding discomfort. This means that we avoid fear at all costs. When I asked Paul what it was that most drew him to a new project, he said it was fear. The work that scared him most was the work he wanted to do. In fact, he said that if the work didn't scare the crap out of him, he didn't do it because fear was the key ingredient in making great television (or great anything). Ray Winstone said a similar thing to me when we were filming *Bouncer*. He said he liked doing the work that frightened him. The challenge to him and to Paul was not in just facing down the fear, but in using the fear as alchemistic base metal to make gold.

Most of us walk around thinking that we are the only people in the world who feel fear. Because of this we avoid things that frighten us, which means we stop growing. People like Paul and Ray are what the poet Rumi called 'night-travellers', people who go into the night and hunt down their fears. They do this because (as Rumi said) the moon shines on night-travellers. Light and knowledge are given to those brave enough to turn and face their fears. The people who see red lights as green, those who lean into the sharp edges are the very people that become ultra successful. It is not that these people do not feel fear. They feel it just the same, sometimes even more acutely than everyone else. It is only that they change their perception of fear. They learn to love the adrenalin and they turn that raw energy into success.

So, what it is that you are avoiding? What is it that you fear?

Maybe now is the time to be brave and turn into the dark, take a step towards it, creep up on it, break off its four corners or – if you are really courageous – dive into it head first and see what happens. You might be surprised to find that fear is not the enemy you always thought it to be. You may be even more surprised to find that buried within that fear is a golden nugget of information that can't be found anywhere else on this earth.

Start now. Be brazen. Be brave. Make the decision. And when the fear rears its ugly head, look it in the eye and dare it to do its worst. Then watch your three-dimensional demon turn into a two-dimensional cartoon and quickly disappear. Fear feeds on your terror. It is nourished by those who turn and run. Courage is the killer of weeds like fear. When you stand and endure, that molten metal of fear inside you turns to gold.

Be a night-traveller!

Chapter 15

Reciprocal Returns

The lad that was visiting my master class was young, maybe 22, and very fit. He knew his way around the mat as far as the ground work was concerned but he was getting tapped out again and again by a succession of my instructors. Not only was he getting tapped out, he was completely out of his depth. I could tell by his face (dispirited), his gait (shoulders hunched, defeated walk) and his eyes (they hit the ground like dropped marbles) that he'd expected a little more of himself. He knew (he later confided) that my class was tough and that the fighters were top drawer but he thought he might at least be able to hold his own.

After the session he asked me where he had gone wrong. To be frank, I wasn't sure. I watched him fight three or four times and all I could see was that he was out-gunned by better players than himself. I couldn't quite put my finger on why there was such a disparity between his ability and that of my people. I was confused so I decided to do a bit of probing.

'How often do you train?' I asked, hoping that his training routine might shed some light on the issue. 'Oh,' he replied (a little too keenly) 'I train twice a week. Without fail.' I remember thinking: Twice a week! Without fail!

I smiled, 'Well that's your problem.' I told him, 'You are training twice a week, these guys are training twice a day. By Monday night they've already done your week's quota of training.'

My visiting martial artist was making the same mistake as many. He was training recreationally and expecting professional results. This is a bit like planting cabbage in your garden and expecting roses in the summer. This problem does not just confine itself to the martial arts. I see the same attitude in all walks of life. Fair-weather golfers who get their clubs out every summer and then wonder why their handicap remains a handicap. Footballers who train on a Wednesday and play on a Sunday but dream of kicking a premiership ball in front of 50,000 screaming fans on a Saturday afternoon. Painters who imagine that three hours at the easel is going to turn them into the next David Hockney. The writing world (similarly) is full of part-time hacks that throw out a weekend script and then bitch because Hollywood does not recognise their genius.

This (I have found) is a universe that gives out what it gets in. The returns are entirely reciprocal. This is good news and bad. Good because it means that anyone who invests their time diligently can expect great returns; bad news because those that want to change what they are getting without changing what they are giving have a lot of stepping up to do.

I am amazed by the amount of people I see who are treading water, banging in the minimal investment and then sitting around waiting for the floodgates of great returns to open up for them. People want gain without pain, profit without investment and reward without risk. And when it doesn't materialise they look outside of themselves and blame.

The law of reciprocal returns is very exciting. It means that you can have anything if you are prepared to do the work and handle the pressure. And its mandate is very clear:

Step up, or shut up!

Chapter 16

Suffering

We are all suffering. There is a fair chance that you are suffering right now and are looking for balm, something – a word, an idea, a sentence, a premise, a medicine, maybe a chant – that might help ease your pain. As a man that has suffered a lot I am no different to anyone else. I want to understand the nature of my suffering and replace it with a heavy dose of peace. If I can't do this, if my suffering is unavoidable, then I at least want to make sense of it. I want my suffering to be for a reason. My sojourn on this globe is not a long one, maybe one century if I am blessed, so I don't really want to spend any of it suffering unless I can profit from the experience. We can all endure suffering if we know why. Nietzsche said that if we know the why we can endure almost anything.

In my bid for knowledge, I (like most) left my city, left my country, actually even left my body in search of the pain panacea. Outside, in books or conversations with gurus, I found no such relief (other than the temporary inspiration that good information affords). Instead I found direction in the guise of a finger that pointed not East, not to the temples of Tibet or the churches of Rome, but back to Coventry, back to my house, my garden, my body. Deeper still, it pointed back to that dark nothingness that pervades all things when I close my eyes.

Every time I go out I am directed back in. Every time I try to run I am encouraged to wait and see. Every time I hide I am advised to try visibility instead. Go inside. Have a good look at the discomfort that resides there. Why? Because suffering is the body's way of telling us that something is wrong. And if we keep covering the message with artificial blankets (painkillers, drink, drugs, sex, denial) we might never know what the suffering means. That never knowing could kill us, or worse still, it could lead us into a long life of unnecessary pain.

From my limited understanding, there are two kinds of suffering. The suffering that we inflict on ourselves, and the suffering that is inflicted up on us by circumstance.

The suffering that we bring on ourselves, we should (if at all possible) eradicate. There is no joy and little gain in suffering unnecessarily. To stop this kind of suffering, we need clinical self-honesty. Nearly all suffering can be traced back to the self. If you are really honest, if you own everything, if you place yourself at cause and expect nothing from anyone, and if you can stop your negative thoughts, most of your suffering will end.

No one can offend us, no one can let us down, no one can abandon us, disappoint us, make us jealous, cheat us, make us envious, angry, greedy, depressed, poor, under-educated, fat or unfit. These are all circumstances that we readily accept, perhaps because we do not know any better, perhaps because we are too lazy to change.

Do we enjoy being a martyr to our suffering?

At one time or another I have fallen into all of these categories. But I have since learned to recognise that I am the centre of my universe. The responsibility for my health, wealth and happiness lies not with the hospitals and doctors, not with the government and certainly not with other people. The moment we rely on outside forces for our well-being, we become their prisoners.

The responsibility lies with you.

If your suffering is health related, why not make it your life's mission to understand your body; find out how to get well and stay well. Become an expert, do a degree, an MA, a PHD; become the most knowledgable person on the planet with regards to your health.

If your suffering is economic, who do you think is going to change your situation if you don't? There is no one coming to your rescue. There are no more heroes. Study economics, put yourself into an apprenticeship with the wealthy and the rich. Study business and make yourself a man of great economic knowledge. The information is all out there, much of it free. Don't blame any outside forces. Don't blame the government because of the poor minimum wage. Don't blame the conglomerates for stealing too much of the pie. Blame is the predictable response of the masses and once employed it knows no end. So get out there, earn your worth and ease your suffering.

If your suffering is mental, make it your life's work to understand the cerebral schematic and put that information to work for you. In fact, make that information public so that you not only ease your own suffering, you ease the suffering of all those who find themselves in your situation. Scour the internet, invest in books, lectures and courses. Talk to the psychologically robust, ask them their secrets, then put that information into use and be the proof that it works.

These options are open to everyone. But information will not drop out of the sky. You need to hunt it down. It can be done. It has been done. History is brimming with folks that have taken responsibility for their own suffering and have not only succeeded in easing their pain, but have become massively successful at the same time.

Austrian neurologist Viktor Frankl said that all suffering is relative. Whether you are lying in bed sweating and manically depressed at three a.m., or you are a Holocaust survivor (like him), your suffering will feel as though it knows no depths. It has been proven by psychologists that the symptoms of manic depression can be as frightening to the sufferer as climbing out of a dug-out with a bayonet to engage in mortal combat.

What I have learned from my suffering is that I don't like it much. But if I can't get out of it immediately, I am going to learn as much from it as I can. Much of the greatest stuff I have learned in the last 46 years has come directly from periods of suffering. In fact, I would say that personal development is a natural by-product of enduring pain, that is, if you are wise enough to look inside rather than outside.

The Sufi poet Rumi said that the chickpea only got its flavour from being boiled in the pot. When it tried to jump out to escape its suffering, the cook pushed it back in with the ladle and said, 'You think I'm torturing you. I'm not. I am boiling you to make you sweet.'

When we are suffering, we all tend to look for an escape. If there is a way out, my recommendation is that you take it. But heed the advise on offer. Your suffering wants you to see something. Do not turn away. Address it. Right now if you can. If you don't, you will find yourself back in the middle of your suffering, again and again, until you get it. Once you are in possession of the vital information you need, leave your suffering behind. Take responsibility, make decisions, change and adapt. Do what is necessary, but leave it behind.

Sometimes you can't.

In these circumstances, Frankl suggests doing something radical. My experiences have led me to the same conclusion. You must be worthy of your suffering. Handle it. He said that there is great liberty in suffering, that we have the opportunity in our darkest moments to reach a higher consciousness through endurance. It is an opportunity offered to few people. This doesn't mean that you just accept suffering, but you endure it stoically while actively looking for a solution.

Pain is a great adviser. Suffering is wise counsel. If you are brave enough to look closely at them, they offer you great secrets. The answer is always hidden within the problem.

If you go into your pain, if you are brave enough to do that, to sit in it and examine it minutely, then the self-inflicted suffering will disappear (because it only feeds on fear). Your life-imposed suffering can offer you transcendence.

Suffering ceases to be suffering when we truly lose our fear of suffering. No one can help you with this. It's up to you. Once you take responsibility for yourself, you will draw assistance from every living corner of the universe.

Chapter 17

The Art of Restriction

When I first started working as a club doorman all those years ago, the thing that struck me most (scared the shit out of me actually) was how restrictive a real confrontation is when it comes to space. It didn't seem to matter whether you were fighting on four acres of mown grass or three-square-feet of pissy pub toilet, the fight always ended up very close and personal. There was rarely any room for manoeuvre.

This is why (and when) I started to experiment with very close range combat. I specialised in punching, because punching is the range most consistently available in a real fight and, culturally, pugilism suited me. I realised way back then that in a fight you very rarely had more than 18 inches of space to work in. Yet all around me there were martial artists practising in a range of three feet or more and using techniques that would not be possible in a live encounter. To try to mend this gaping hole in contemporary combat, for me and for anyone else interested in taking it to the concrete, I developed what I called 'restrictive training.'

By using this technique I was able to summon instant power from any position and at any range, even the most restrictive. Whether I was in a car or a phone booth, a toilet cubicle or a farmer's field, I was able to draw an explosion of power from (seemingly) nothing. I encouraged my students to punch from seated positions (floor, chair, etc.), kneeling positions; from on their backs, their bellies, with their backs against the wall – from anywhere that massively restricted their movements. From restricted positions you are unable to employ hip twist or use momentum to garner power. This restriction forces you to 'find' something else. And you do. Very quickly.

Because of restriction of movement and space, we started to develop massive relaxation through necessity. When you have no range of movement, tension and stiffness completely impede any power. We started to employ joints (the more the better) in the technique, so that (for instance) if I was in a phone booth or a toilet cubicle or on a packed dance floor, I could summon tremendous power and explosion without even moving my feet. And then there was intent, one of the first things that starts to grow when space is at a premium. You realise very quickly that intent of power is power. Then there is that certain something that only restriction training can develop, an indefinable energy, an explosion at the end of the technique that cannot be brought or bartered. You won't find it in a book or on a tape or even in a class. The Chinese call it 'chi,' the Japanese 'qui.' It has as many names as there are cultures. Personally I don't want to place a name to it or throw a shroud of mystique around it. I can't claim to know what the energy is other than an accident. Restrictive training helps you to become accident prone. It works so well that folks have to start pulling their punches because the power they are generating is too much for their bones (they start picking up injuries) and too much for the bones of their opponents. Not only does restrictive training force people to find some other source of power than the one that they normally employ, it also acts as an accelerator; people become big hitters much faster than normal. It would be no exaggeration to say that I get people punching twice as hard within one session using this method.

But being able to punch hard is not what excites me about restrictive training.

What I really love about it is the fact that it enables you to view life restrictions from a totally different and positive perspective. Just as restriction can trigger the release of chi in physical training so can restriction in life (if viewed correctly) enable you to discover a reservoir of hitherto untapped power.

Lance Armstrong was given a life-threatening restriction called cancer. He had a choice. Lie down and take it and probably die within a year, or find something that would not only enable him to heal, but also give him the power to win the Tour de France an unprecedented eight times. Do you know that he was so dominant in the Tour that the organisers changed the route several times to give the other riders a chance at winning?

I was bullied at school and suffered badly from depression. I had a choice. Accept this and live a life of mediocrity and fear, or find something inside me, some force, some power that would not only elevate me above my playground tormentors, but also take me to the world stage in martial arts and in writing.

Everyone reading this is restricted in one way or another. It might be a health issue or a relationship problem, it might be money or fear. Your restriction could be that you are without direction or hope. If you are like most people (I hope you are not), you are probably looking outside of yourself for someone to blame. If you have the courage to stop projecting and look inside youself you might be surprised to find that there is an infinite amount of power available to you within the very restriction you are trying to escape.

Many people (I count myself as one of them) go into life and search out restriction in order that they might grow. They seek out tough martial arts schools where they are at the bottom of the class, difficult jobs where they feel out of their depth, situations that scare them, places (inside and out) that expose their cracks. Some people are really brave and restrict themselves with the little things that make the biggest difference – things like diet, personal discipline, counselling, and psychotherapy. Others (and I also include myself in this group) have no need to go in search of restriction because restriction has been thrust upon them by illness, money or family problems. Either way, your route to the stars is not to turn your back on restriction and kick and scream and wish it gone, but rather it is to turn into it, grab your spade of courage and dig deep. Somewhere within the problem you are facing right now is the answer that you have been looking for your whole life.

Chapter 18

The Blame Trap

As a species we have the power to change the world (certainly our own world). Of this I have no doubt. In fact, I am the living embodiment of my 'live-it-now and do-it-all' philosophy. I live my life in the creation business. I create my world. I love every minute of it. Thus far I have managed to make manifest every desire I have set my intention on. This is not meant to sound smug. I see myself as a very ordinary person who has managed to liberate himself from a life of unnecessary toil. If I can do it, believe me, anyone can.

I measure my accomplishment not by the balance in my bank (though lots of noughts can be very pleasing), but by the fact that when I get up in the morning and when I go to bed at night, I feel happy. That's what makes me a success.

As a child I always dreamed of making my living as a writer. As an adult that is exactly what puts bread on my table from one day to the next. Success, of course, is very subjective. Your idea of nirvana may be – and very likely is – entirely different from mine. As long as what you do makes you happy then it would be fair to say you are a success. It's when you spend your life doing the things you don't like that the Monday morning feeling stretches through until Friday afternoon and Sundays are a dread because they precede Monday. That's when you find yourself thinking, 'Is this what I really want to do with my life?' This is especially true if you feel you have no other choice.

People are forever telling me that they would love to write, to sculpt, to garden, or to teach but they can't because their life, their wife, the mortgage, the kids, their environment, their circumstances – even God – won't allow it. This very statement, one I used (to death) as a younger man, is a self-fulfilling prophecy. It is probably the most over-used and certainly the most disempowering combination of words you could ever make the mistake of employing. It does exactly what it says on the tin. If you can't do what you want to do because you wife says so, you give her all your power. That means that until she says yes, you're stuck where you are. If you blame the environment, circumstance or your upbringing, you give all your power over to these inanimates. And, again, it means that, until they favour you, you're glued to mediocrity. If you believe you are powerless (the moment you fall into the blame trap you *are* powerless), then by definition you are exactly that.

The reason I know this is because I have fallen into the same trap more times than I care to remember. As a fledgling, I spent my days wallowing in procrastination, blame and self-pity. I hated my lot but, of course, my lot was never my fault (is it ever?)

The answer is as simple as a Greek drama. Take back the responsibility for your own creative power. Admit ownership of your future then set about building a palatial existence that makes you happy, and by extension, makes all those you love happy also. It takes bollocks of cast-iron to take the reins but if you want to trail-blaze then riding shotgun is not where it's at.

Think about the job you do for one moment. You probably spend two thirds (at least) of your waking life at work. Two-thirds! Now if you don't love the bones off your job, if you are not inspired to the point of exhilaration about the nuts and bolts of your current employment, if they don't have to drag you away from the office kicking and screaming at the end of each day because you want to do more, then you have to ask yourself, 'Why am I there?' Just hope that your first answer is not, 'The money!'

I am emphatic about this message so please don't think me conceited when I tell you that I love my life. I love being me. It wasn't always this way. I spent the first half of my life living other people's idea of normal. I hated it to pieces. Now I enjoy my life so much I don't want to sleep at night. I want to be out there experiencing everything.

You see, when you love what you do it stops being work and becomes fun. My working life is unconventional certainly, unpredictable definitely, and sometimes it scares the living shit out of me, for sure. But I like unconventional. I thrive on the unpredictability and (if I am being honest here), I like being scared. I love being overwhelmed, even out of my depth. I have become comfortable with discomfort because discomfort is a sign that I am growing. I don't want to be stuck in the middle of some cornflake-size comfort zone, sweeping around a metaphoric lathe. I want to be precariously balanced on some craggy precipice where I can see it all.

'Yea, I agree,' you might say, 'but (the obligatory BUT) it's really hard.'

Of course it's hard, it has to be hard. You can't temper a blade without putting it through a forge. What's the use of a blue ribbon when you haven't even run the race? It is difficult, but please, let's keep things in perspective here. Carrying a hod on a building site is back-breakingly hard, working your brain into mush on a computer everyday can be hard with a capital H. Any job, especially the ones you despise, that entails bargaining two-thirds of your life just to make the mortgage is harder than a big bag of hard things. We all know about hard. It's what we do on a daily basis. At least when your sweat is vocational, when you are hacking away in the right jungle, you can sit down at the end of another satisfying day and think, 'This is what I really want to do with my life.'

We are where we are in life through choice. (Oh yes we are, even if it is just the fact that we do not choose to change where we are.) If we don't like it, we have the God-given power to reinvent ourselves. The moment we think that we lack this power our thoughts make it so.

Someone dead famous (so famous I can't remember his name) once said (and he was right), 'If you think you can or you think you can't, you are right.'

Chapter 19

The Pornographic Wasp

If I told you that it was a wasp that taught me the dangers of pornography you'd probably accuse me of being a honeycomb short of the full hive, but it is true. Before I recount the lesson, I have a confession to make. I do like pornography.

Actually that is not entirely accurate.

Let's say that I am highly aroused by pornography.

I don't really like it because, well, like all addictions, it drains my energy. Sometimes it completely disempowers me. I am highly aroused by it because it is innate, it is my genes. So I don't watch it anymore. I don't read it. In fact, I don't entertain it at all. I haven't for many years. I let it go around about the same time that I stopped drinking alcohol. But I don't judge it either. I don't like porn because it is an addiction and addictions are prisons for the weak of will. I won't be weak neither will I be prisoner to my senses. I want to be strong and I want to be free. So my issue with pornography is neither a moral nor ethical one. For me, it is all about mastering my body and mind through the control of self (all growth starts with the self). The first and best and most immediate way to control the self is via the senses, and I tackled (and continue to tackle) my senses through the deliberate slaughter of my addictions. The Kabbalah teaches us that all our power, all our wealth is locked into our addictions, and when we kill those addictions we win our power back. And when we have our power back we can do anything we like with it.

Those who are heavily addicted are prisoners to their addiction. Killing your addictions opens the door to freedom. (Our main addictions in this society are drugs, alcohol, gambling, pornography and people pleasing. Most people are infected with at least one of these, some people have them all.) It is a trick that I learned from Gandhi, who used this method of abstention to change the course of human history (no less). At the time of his death he had some three hundred million followers. He believed that each of us has one major addiction and that when you closed the door to that one, you closed the door to all your addictions. And when you controlled yourself you literally controlled the world.

This is what my friend the wasp taught me.

Like most people, I convinced myself that a little bit of porn was OK as long as I kept control of it. But with something as powerful as sex (especially for the sexually-profligate male who has about a million years of procreational conditioning in his genes) moderation (I believe) is an untenable philosophy. Like any drug you indulge, each injection needs to be stronger and sooner than the last to get the same buzz. It is small wonder then that people who initially indulge light flirtation with porn quickly progress to the hardcore, often dangerous, mutations that no longer resemble the procreational act of intercourse with a loving partner. I always justified it to myself as 'just something blokes did' until my appetite grew more and more controlling and started to threaten my integrity. It got so that it was difficult for me to walk down the street without checking out (and imagining what I might do with) the curves of every shapely female that happened to pass by. I'd go into book shops to purchase works on philosophy, psychology and spirituality and suddenly find myself in the erotica section flicking though the pages of porn made to look like art. When you find yourself doing things against your own will, you have to start asking yourself a few questions. The question I asked myself was, 'Is this something I can indulge or will it always be an addiction looking for a host?' We all think we can indulge and flirt around the edges of our addictions, but deep down we know that really we can't, because an addiction that is alive is always an addiction that is a threat. Many famous folks have ruined their careers, their health and their relationships because a flirtation with fire set light to their whole lives. I have many friends who have not given their addictions the respect they demand. Their flippancy has (or will) cost them dearly. Some lost their jobs, others their liberty, many their lives. Whilst I am not saying that porn will kill you, I am saying that it will imprison you (whilst letting you think that you are still free).

And this is where the wasp comes in. This is not a metaphor. It is a true story. I sat in my garden drinking a fruit juice and I did what I always do when I need an honest answer. I'd just indulged in a porn fest (even though I really didn't want to) and was feeling... controlled. And weak. Because I no longer felt that I had a choice in the matter. The urge came on. I indulged it. I felt shit afterwards. It had become a habitual cycle. I knew that I wanted to lose this addiction but I just couldn't find enough reason to stop. I kept rationlising and telling myself that 'a little bit won't do you any harm.' Deep down I knew that the little bit was getting bigger and bigger. It needed to be stopped. So I put down the empty glass, closed my eyes and asked for a sign. When I opened my eyes there was a wasp hovering just above my glass. It landed briefly on the glass, stole a residue of my fruit juice and flew away. Within a few brief seconds the wasp was back. He was still being careful; he hovered, landed, had a look around, took a glob of juice from just inside the glass and flew away again. When he returned the third time he was more confident. He flew straight into the glass, took several globs of juice and, when he was ready, flew off. I smiled as I watched the wasp return again and again, each time more confident, each time staying a little longer, each time going a little deeper into the glass and each time drinking in a little more than the last.

Until the final time.

Arrogant now, my wasp flew straight to the bottom of the glass where there was a pool of thick juice. He stood right in the middle of it and drank and drank and – started to drown. He was up to his little knees in juice and could not lift himself back out.

The small indulgence had quickly turned into a life-threatening addiction.

I got the message.

I tipped the glass so that the wasp – having kindly passed on its wisdom to me – could fly away to live another day.

I never indulged my addiction again.

Chapter 20

The Power of Books

To my pleasure, I have discovered the hidden power of books.

What we need to help us rise above the crowd is information. Actually, I stand corrected. I know plenty of people with information by the bucketload but for whatever reason they do not use it. I also know many people who use the information they have, but use it wrongly. Aspiring to achieve wisdom is the correct way to use information. One of the best ways to collect information (and of course inspiration and aspiration) is books. When I spend thousands of pounds on books, I consider it an investment in me, the person most likely to get me where I want to be. In books, we have the opportunity to access the knowledge of a thousand life times and assimilate it until it becomes us. I am the living embodiment of what I have experienced and a big part of what I have experienced has been gained through the medium of reading. I always tell my little lad (when he is struggling to get into a book) that readers are leaders. Small libraries make great men. It is something that I believe emphatically. I have yet to meet a hugely successful person that wasn't a voracious reader. I even took a speed-reading course so that I could get through more material. It's all out there just waiting for you, and if you go to a public library, it's absolutely free.

Can you imagine that, all that knowledge, all the secrets, all that information for the price of a few beers and a curry? I've spent up to £50 on a single book if it was the one that I was looking for. People often say that the only way out of the rat race is through football or sport or pure luck. It's not true. The best way out is through the library. Mention any famous name and I'll almost guarantee that you'll be able to find their whole life – highs, lows, successes, failures, likes and dislikes, and the secrets to their success – between the pages of a library book. Now if that is not offering it all up on a plate for your inspiration, I don't know what is. I find it absolutely incredible that you can go into any bookshop (or even the Internet) and buy the lives of the greatest men and women in history. You can find out why and how single individuals changed the course of history.

One man, William Wallace, witnessed the slaughter of a whole village of people and decided that he was going to do something about it. He told his wife. She said, 'But you're only one man.' That one man changed the course of history with his strength and courage. Have you read about this great and saintly woman, Mother Teresa? She cared for thousands and touched the hearts of millions. Just an ordinary girl who did extraordinary things; a village girl who touched the whole planet. What about the courage of Churchill, the tenacity of Thatcher, the wisdom of the Dalai Lama, the power and love of Sai Baba, the focus and dreams of Bill Gates, the rise and fall of Bonaparte? The list is absolutely endless. And they are all there waiting in books to point you in the right direction. All these extraordinary men and women saying, 'Let me tell you what I've learned in my life.' What an incredible opportunity.

I am sitting here with a book of drawings by Saul Steinberg staring up at me. Steinberg isn't dead; he is alive and kicking in my office. He sat here, alive in his work, saying, 'What can I do for you Geoff? What can I teach you about my life through my work? Ask me, I'm here.' Did you know that Escher lives with me? You're damn right he does! And he only cost me about 20 quid. It was an absolute steal, I have to tell you. A steal. He is here with me now. All his drawings and all his words. When I am feeling a little insecure about my work he is there to help me.

'Listen, Geoff,' he tells me, 'we all feel insecure at times. I went on to become a world-renowned artist but there wasn't a day when I didn't doubt my work. There wasn't a day when I didn't think, "Is this any good?"'

Escher has taught me that insecurity driven into your work is what makes it great. The very fact that the great Escher can doubt his own work, can feel insecure, can feel like giving it all up, makes me feel that I am not on my own and that it is OK to have bad days. An ordinary person can reach the stars. I remember first looking at his work and being filled with awe. I'd never have believed that he would have any insecurities at all about this great art. But in his book he said, 'I've absolutely no reason to moan about the "success" of my work, nor about the lack of ideas for there are plenty of them. And yet I'm plagued by an immense feeling of inferiority, a desperate sense of general failure. Where do these crazy feelings come from?'

I have Gandhi's life story in front of me. The book cost eight pounds. The price was so little that I am almost embarrassed to mention it. I spend more than that on car parking in a single week. Yet this one book has given me more direction and more hope than any amount of money could have. Mr Gandhi has taken me behind the scenes of his life and shown me the rights and the wrongs. He has given me the secret to inner power, he has taught me that faith in yourself and your God means immortality. This also means that nothing is beyond you once you decide to ride the bull. He has shown me that I only have to master one single thing in my life and I can have anything I want. That one single thing is 'me.' Gandhi learned how to lead himself, and he made loads of mistakes along the way. By doing so he built up a personal following of over three hundred million people. Can you imagine that? And reading his book taught me that I could, you could, and we all could do exactly the same thing.

There are only so many things we can learn in one lifetime, only so many lessons we can learn with the finite years that we are allotted. It's not enough time really. That's why books were invented. You can take a thousand great people and learn the lessons they gleaned from their lives. If you discipline yourself and get a lot of reading done, you can become the manifestation of a thousand great people.

Take what it was that made them legendary and make it a part of you. These people have left their stories, their 'instructions for life' so that you can get onto the fast track, so that you don't have to do the thousands of experiments they had to do to learn what they learned. Once you have acquired this knowledge you can use it to power your own journey of discovery. If you wanted to get around London the best thing to do would be to buy a street map.

The biographies of great people are simply that, street maps to life. They have departed to another plane and left you the treasure maps. It's great. It's so wonderful. All you have to do is get out there and buy the books, read the stories, learn the lessons and put them into action.

If you make reading a habit, it'll be the best habit you ever make.

Chapter 21

The Reciprocal Universe

I spoke with a guy the other day who told me that his passion was directing film. He lived and breathed directing. It was all he wanted to do. I knew he was kidding himself. He wasn't directing. He worked a nine-to-five job that bored him completely. He was not a member of any film groups. He did not direct his own films on the weekends. All he did was talk.

Directors do not talk, they direct.

Take Shane Meadows. He wanted to be a director so he got together with a few mates and a camera and directed a bunch of short films that got him noticed. Today he is one of the most respected and sought after directors in Britain.

He wanted to direct so he directed. He did not wait for the grants or the permissions or the favours or the fates. He got a camera, he got his mates and he got busy making films.

That is what directors do.

I have a friend who wants to write. He tells me that he lives and breathes writing. Writing is his life. As soon as his money situation is better, he is going to invest in a course, a computer and maybe a trip to Cannes where he could pitch his film idea and get the funds he needs to sit and write the great work that he has in him. It was only the money that was holding him back, he said.

But it was not the cash that was stopping him. Neither was it the time or the tides. It was simply the fact that he was not a writer because writers write.

Writers do not talk a good script. They sit on their arses and bleed into their computers until they have 120 pages (that will need to be paired painfully down to 90) of carefully crafted prose. Then (after the director, the producer, the actors, the financers, the designer, the tea boy and the runners have read the first draft) they go away and write it again and again and again until it positively shimmers.

I know that my friend is not a real writer because he throws something together over a weekend and blames the fates when it comes back unread and unwanted.

I have another friend (several actually) who wants to make a splash in the world of martial arts. He has something big to say (he says) and the minute the circumstances are right (perhaps next year?) he will say it. He thinks about training in the US with the Machado brothers (but it's too dear). He dreams of going to Brazil to train with the Gracie family (but its too far). He might even do a little stint in Japan (but his wife isn't keen). If only he was as lucky as me and was able to give up his job and train full-time he felt sure that he could hit the world stage.

But he knows deep down (as I know) that the circumstances will never quite favour him. There will never be enough money to purchase tutelage from the Gracies, Brazil will always be too far a trip and his wife will never agree to Japan. And this is not because any of these things are not possible, but because my friend does not really want them enough. He is not really a martial artist with something big to say to the world. He is just a man with a bag of excuses that get ever more diverse and inventive.

Martial artists train, with the best folks on the planet, whenever and wherever they can. They live and they breathe it. They create their own favour, they find the money, the time, the permission. They move with such force that the whole universe is forced to react and create their dream. The universe is touch-sensitive to our intentions. Let me tell you that it does not wait for tomorrow, next week or next year.

It waits only for you.

So let me ask you this: When are you going to make a move? When are you going to command the fates to do your bidding? When are you going to wave your baton of intention and orchestrate the universe? Don't wait like the masses for tomorrow; it does not exist.

Now is the time to act. Book yourself on that directing course you always wanted to do. Start the writing class that has been in your mind forever. Set a deadline date to make your first film. Sit and write, go and run. Whatever it is that you have been dreaming of, make it real now, before you, like the millions before, become the dust of a generation that died with their best music still in them.

And if you are scared, if the very thought of acting makes you quiver with fear; GOOD.

Discomfort is good.

All growth has a kernel of discomfort, a red light for the majority, but for the minority – those with spunk and drive and ambition – discomfort is a green light.

But nothing will move until you move. Nutrients do not mobilise until the seed of intention is planted, fate does not shape circumstance without action, serendipity only manifests when we take up our positions and act.

Jump and a net will appear.

Chapter 22

There is No Land Rover

'There is no Land Rover. There is no Land Rover. There is… NO LAND ROVER.'

I say it over and over again in my mind with the rhythm of a metronome.

'There is no Land Rover.'

It keeps me sane. It keeps me on track. It stops me from being fooled into resting up and celebrating too soon, loosening my helmet straps before the fight is won.

'There is no Land Rover. There is no… '

I suppose I should explain what I'm talking about before you get to thinking that me and my glassy-smooth marbles have parted company.

Picture the scene. You are on selection for the SAS. You've just hiked goodness knows how many miles over the icy, toe-blackening Brecon Beacons on little more than a Mars Bar and the promise that 'when you see the Land Rover, you're home. Jump in the back, take off your boots, have yourself a brew.'

So all the way around, over hills and valleys, past the graves of former aspirants, walking on blisters, working around strains and cuts and injuries, hovering somewhere between breathlessness and total exhaustion, living on fresh air and a frozen chocolate bar, total collapse an ever present vulture on your left shoulder, utter failure an odds-on favourite on your right... and then you see it. Like a watery oasis in a dry desert.

The Land Rover.

Home.

You smile for the first time in days. You quicken your pace. Your mind rushes forward to a hot tea, maybe some food and bed. But just as you get within a few feet of your golden carriage, it drives off leaving you stranded and confused and distraught – and fooled. The sergeant (dressed in a warm coat, sipping a hot tea) tells you to continue on. When you ask him, 'How much further,' he gives you one of those wry smiles and says, 'Until you see the Land Rover.'

Most people, at this point, do not continue on. They take an imaginary towel and throw it into the ring of metaphor. They have been tricked, and (for the majority) that trick is enough to kill their dream.

It has beaten them. They only placed enough fuel in the tank to get them to the Land Rover, and not beyond. Not even a foot beyond. For those who do manage to pick themselves up and continue (for an added and unspecified distance), there is instant enlightenment.

'There is no Land Rover.'

And that becomes their mantra. Until they are literally sitting inside the vehicle of choice with a hot tea, the Land Rover does not exist.

There is no Land Rover.

Especially when everyone around you is telling you that there is.

I remember this every time I think a script is going to be optioned (definitely this time), a battle is going to finish (imminently) or a big deal is as good as done (just 't's to cross and 'i's to dot). I have seen many strong fighters beaten just at the point where they thought victory was certain. I've lost count of friends who have celebrated a deal before that all important eleventh hour. Regretfully, I had friends who lost their lives when they loosened their helmet straps because they believed that the enemy had retreated and the fight was (as good as) won.

So many people fall for the Land Rover trick and give up just short of greatness because they allow themselves to believe that the Land Rover exists. Well, it does exist, sort of, but only when you've got your arse on the seat, and the tea in your hand. Until then is it little more than a phantom. It is healthy to remember this if you intend to reach the top in any game because (believe me) that big deal is always looming. The Land Rover is always 'just over the next hill.'

When the film is on screen, when the cheque is in the bank (and has cleared) and when the back door is bolted and secured, I take my celebratory beverage because that is the only time the Land Rover is real.

Until then there is no Land Rover.

And that will remain my mantra.

Chapter 23

They Laughed at Lowry

Excitedly I phoned a friend to tell him my news. I'd just won an international development award for my film script *Clubbed* (based on my book *Watch My Back*); I had to tell someone. It's what you do when providence lights your day. 'Oh, I see,' he said half-scoffing, half laughing, 'I suppose it'll be the Oscars next then?' His attitude landed like a heavy right. There was bitterness in his tone that made me regret the call.

'Well yea,' I replied (a bit too defensively), 'if that's what I intend to do then why not? Why not! There's a guy in Preston, Nick Park, who's won four!' (If I have to I'll go and get one of his!)

After replacing the receiver, still reeling from his unexpected response, I assured myself that my friend's attitude need not ruin my day, and I should never let him, or any others, hold me back. Criticism, cynicism and jealousy are a familiar trinity, often encountered when leaving a muddy comfort zone en route to a starry ideal. I wasn't the first to be laughed at for daring to dream, neither would I be the last.

When a young German climber told his friends of his bold intentions to climb the perilous mountain Nanga Parbat solo – a feat never before attempted, let alone achieved – they didn't just laugh at him. They called him insane. Equally insane was the idea that two inexperienced men (with an investment of only $30 and a penchant for good ice cream) could one day take on confectionary giant Hagen Das. Reinhold Messner climbed Nanga Parbat solo only six weeks after conquering Everest without oxygen. Ben & Jerry turned their $30 investment into a billion dollar, giant-slaying industry. Who's laughing now?

And they laughed at Lowry, too, you know. When the painter L.S. Lowry first placed his oils to canvas, the haughty elite of the contemporary art world held their chuckling bellies and laughed the gentle northerner out of Manchester. They slandered him at every opportunity for trying to be more than (they thought) he was. They called him an amateur and his work (at best) naïve. 'Who (they asked) does he think he is?' Later, when the (so-called) mighty had crumbled under the might and beauty of Lowry's vision, and his genius shone through the oils (bidders eventually paid millions to own one of his originals), Lowry had the last laugh. His later exhibitions were dedicated to 'the men who laughed at Lowry.' Manchester opened *The Lowry Galleries* to honour his work.

I love that! Don't you love that? All of us have at one time or another had our ideas stamped on, scoffed at or laughed about – often by those closest to us. All of us have watched the uncouth kick our dreams around the floor like cola cans. I love the Lowry story because I have been the butt of many an unkind 'who does he think he is' jibe when I dared to swim against the societal stream. I can take solace in the fact that they laughed at Lowry. He became global, not only in spite of his detractors, but also perhaps because of them.

I can well remember being bored to depression in the distant past and thinking, 'There must be more to life than this.' Seeking answers, I turned to my workmate at the factory – elbow-deep in suds, nails full of shit – and said to him, 'There's got to be more to life than this.' He laughed at me, then leaning forward (as though about to tell me a secret), he winked at me (as wise old veterans are inclined to do), 'This is your lot,' he said, 'you should be grateful. This is a job for life.'

It was the job-for-life bit that scared the tripe out of me. I think he could tell by the way my jaw went slack and my eyes hit the floor like marbles that his shop-floor philosophy had failed to enlighten me. What he said next – not just the words, but the bitterness and conviction with which he delivered them – didn't either. It was like a dry slap across the gob.

'You'll still be here when you're 60.'

Shortly after my tête-à-tête with Plato-of-the-lathe, I snapped my broom (very symbolic) and left the factory forever, never to return. All the things I wanted to do, things I was told I could not – I did. And more. And I am still doing them. This is my life, I can do anything, go anywhere, be whomever I want. We all can. And for those that laugh at my dreams, watch out!

They laughed at Lowry. And look what happened to him.

Chapter 24

Time

My first book was written whilst sitting on the toilet in a factory that employed me to sweep floors, so you can imagine the fun I have when people comment – on finding out that I am a writer – 'Of course I'd love to write a book but I haven't got the time.' Invariably, their faces scrunch into question marks when I ask, 'Is there a toilet where you work?'

Not that I recommend the loo as the healthiest environment to write your latest – or indeed first – bestseller, far from it. In fact, after six months of sitting on the throne writing, I now suffer loss of feeling in my lower legs and a permanent red ring around my bum. I am just making the point that if you have the will you'll always find a way, but if you haven't, or you harbour any doubts or fears, then lack of time will always be a convenient excuse not to live your dreams.

When I wrote my first book I was doing two jobs and bringing up a family. I wanted desperately to write a book. I was fully committed to writing it. And, hey, I found the time. But by the same count, whenever I failed to fully commit myself to a goal – and there were many such occasions – or when I did not place my heart in the driving seat, 'time' was not forthcoming and the vehicle refused to move.

The next convenient excuse (believe me I have used them all) that people lean towards is lack of facility. (Do you have a toilet where you work?) Granted, at some point in your development, tools and facilities will be important and lack of them can hold you back, but that's no excuse for not starting out, and certainly no pretext for not succeeding. Pelé, arguably the greatest football player of all time, honed his ball skill kicking coconuts barefoot (ouch!) on the beach. Many a thriving, multi-million- (even multi-billion-) pound business was started from a rickety garden shed held together by chunks of work ethic and a set of hand-me-down, elbow-greased tools. A great proportion of successful entrepreneurs built their conglomerates out of cottage industry. Many godzillionaires made their fortunes not only despite their handicaps but also because of them. Richard Branson's first office was a public phone booth. He had no facilities and no money, but he did have a forceful desire that attracted success and convinced bank managers to hand over the readies without a security or reference in sight.

Do you realise how many genius ideas are lost when the moment is not seized, and how many are stolen while people stand in the shadow of trepidation? For instance, it is thought that some of the greatest writers of each generation never see their name in print and are never published. And it's not because prospective publishers turn down their work, rather it is because the authors never send their work to them. Or even worse, they never actually write it in the first place.

All my early work was hand-written and in severe conditions that did not lend themselves to my quest. Until I could afford a word processor (later a computer) my working tools consisted of one blue biro (with perfunctory chewed top) and a lined, ring-bound reporter's pad kindly donated by the factory stores. I had no time, no machine with fail-safe grammar and spell check – unless you count my wife who kept saying things like, 'You've spelt that wrong' – and no hefty commission-carrot tempting the words from my often uncooperative unconscious. My only incentive, my driving force, was the dread of having to work in the factory for the rest of my life.

The only thing I did have that set me apart from the crowd was desire. Whilst I may have lacked the contemporary tools of the scribe and my writing quarters were certainly not ideal (one might say that they were piss-poor), I did desperately want to write. My want was always greater than my lack. Once you have desire and you totally commit yourself to the process it is almost as though the whole universe conspires to make it happen. Those who don't make the commitment rarely, if ever, make the grade. And I know how hard it can be. I am sympathetic to family and work commitments. I brought up four children so I know all about responsibility. But as I said, time is very malleable, it can be stretched, it accommodates committed souls, those searching for the grail of achievement. Paradoxically, time can be cruel; it will be gone forever, never to be seen again, if we fail to use it profitably. We immortalise our time when we invest every second, minute and hour in the present.

And I figure that when it comes to using our time we would be wise to recognise that we are all allotted the same amount. Branson and Gates only get 24 hours a day. It is what we do with our time that determines where our lives may lead. For me it means getting up early and going to bed late. It also means sacrificing some of the little things that act as time-eating termites. But above all it means refraining from using the time-honoured excuse, 'I haven't got time' because you have. Really! In my experience, 'haven't-got-the-time' is just a pseudonym for 'haven't-got-the-will'. You'll always fit in more if 'more' is preceded by a no-excuses personal commitment to making it happen. If you want something enough, and I mean really want it with your heart and soul, nothing will stop you, nothing will get in your way.

You don't have to look far to see the people that don't make that commitment. They're the ones sitting in the factory canteen bemoaning their existence and blaming the world for their lack. I was once one of them. Now I make a commitment. For many reasons. Not least because I refuse to be a 90-something coffin dweller spending my days regretting the things that I failed to do.

Chapter 25

Waterfall

You know how it is sometimes. You are going through an emotional stretch and things feel a little (or a lot) dark. You feel sort of needlessly tortured. I figure it is simply a purgatory situated somewhere between the edge of our comfort zones and freedom that we will continue to visit as long as we continue to grow. I do hope so. As uncomfortable as it might be I know that without adversity there will be no advance. And who would want that?

I was there again recently actually. In that dark void. Life had cornered me with a heavy dose of highly-challenging workload and unexpected family illness. I was as vulnerable as the lobster shedding its shell. So I did what I often do between the night and day of personal transformation. I went for a walk in the local country park to see if nature had any lessons to offer, something that might rub a little balm across my throbbing brow. Nature has many lessons. In fact much of what I have learned thus far about pain has been through observing how (as the Bible says) the lilies in the field neither spin nor toil.

But today nature was not forthcoming. Nothing I observed offered any solace. Until, that is, I hit the last five minutes of my walk and stood on a bridge that acted as both a crossing point to a small stream and an observation platform to a beautiful little waterfall. It had been raining heavily all week and, as a consequence, the waterfall was gushing over the precipice into the stream below. The turmoil of the fall seemed to exactly mirror the internal struggle that I was experiencing, raging and seemingly uncontrollable emotions that were racing through my mind and body with an energy that I did not recognise as my own. Then I intuited something else, something that gave me the inspiration that I was looking for.

I noticed that in the stream immediately after the fall the water was very deep. In fact the deepest part of the whole stream was right there. Immediately after the fall. I liked this observation. It helped me to realise and understand that after adversity, the Niagara that all of us experience during difficult times, a deeper more profound understanding could be found. I stretched back in my mind and realised that my greatest life lessons thus far, the reference points that helped me to negotiate ever new and ever burgeoning challenges, had always been born out of hard times. The good stuff that I wrote about in my books, talked about in my videos/podcasts and dramatised in my films and plays was the fruit of the hard harvests that life had given me. Then I looked further along the stream, on the other side of the bridge, and I noticed that the water there was very calm. This told me something too. It told me that even the most violent storms do not last forever, and that after adversity there is always peace; after great darkness comes great light. This gave me hope. At the time I desperately needed it. Often when we are in the very middle of a crisis our pain feels infinite and without end. My observations told me that no single feeling can last forever. As I continued to watch (and this is completely true) I noticed a duck swimming down the stream. It didn't seem to notice that about ten feet in front of it the waterfall was at full rage. I wondered how the duck might deal with it. I watched and observed and was amazed to see that a few feet away from the waterfall the duck simply lifted itself out of the water, flew above the waterfall and landed safely on the other side of the bridge where the waters were calm. Amazing. What I loved about this was the fact that the raging waterfall was still there, the duck just chose to rise above it. It did not attach to the turmoil below.

I walked away with my first smile in weeks, determined to no longer attach to my pain, knowing that my understanding would deepen because of my experience and that there was a heavy dose of calm coming my way sometime soon.

Chapter 26

We Are All Dying

I have some good news and some bad news for you (as the joke goes). The bad news – and I'm very sorry to be the bearer – is that we are all dying. It's true. I've checked it out. In fact, I've double- and triple-checked it. I've had it substantiated and, well, there's no easy way to say it, we are dying. It's something that I always kind of knew, but never really chose to think about too much. But the fact is, within the next 70 or 80 years – depending on how old you are and how long you last – we are all going to be either coffin dwellers or trampled ash in the rose garden of some local cemetery. We may not even last that long. After all, we never quite know when the hooded, scythe-carrying, bringer-of-the-last-breath might come-a-calling. It could be sooner than we'd like. I have watched death from the sidelines, quite recently in fact, and nothing underlines the uncertainty and absolute frailty of humanity like the untimely exit of a friend.

Scary.

Now that I have depressed you, here's the good news. Knowing that we are all budding crypt-kickers takes away all the uncertainty of life. We already know how the story ends. The prologue and epilogue are already typed in. All that's left is the middle bit and that's down to us. We get to choose the meat of the story.

So, all those plans that you have on the back burner, you know, the great things you're going to do with your life 'when the time is right?' Well, the time is never quite right, I find. It needs to be brought forward and done now, this minute, pronto, in a hurry, as quick as your little legs will carry you. The novel that you want to write, the trip to the Grand Canyon you've always planned to take, your mind's-eye dream-job, the West End play you want to direct – you have to do them now. We're dying, see. It's official.

So putting your dreams on the back burner until the circumstances are right means that they'll probably never be realised. Our only regrets in life are the things we don't do. We owe it to ourselves to go out and do them now before it's too late. Tomorrow? It's all a lie; there isn't a tomorrow. There's only a promissory note that we are often not in a position to cash. It doesn't even exist. When you wake up in the morning it'll be today again and all the same rules will apply. Tomorrow is just another version of now, an empty field that will remain so unless we start planting some seeds. Your time, which is ticking away as we speak (at about 60 seconds a minute chronologically; a bit faster if you don't invest your time wisely) will be gone and you'll have nothing to show for it but regret and a rear-view mirror full of 'could haves', 'should haves' and 'would haves'.

Have you ever noticed when you go to a buffet restaurant how they give you a bowl the size of a saucer and then say, 'Have as much salad as you like but you can only go up once.' Life is like that small salad bowl. Like the hungry people waiting for their main course, we can cram as much into that tiny bowl as we can carry. I love watching people ingeniously stack the cucumber around the side of the bowl – like they're filling a skip – and then cramming it so high that they have to hire a fork-lift truck to get it back to the table. They're not greedy. They just know that they only have one shot at it.

Fill your bowl. We come this way but once so let's make the best of the short stay. Like the once-a-year holiday to Florida or Spain. Fit as much into the short time there as you can. Make sure that you go back home knackered because you got so much done.

If you don't want to be a postman then don't be a postman. Give it up and be a painter, a writer, a tobogganist, whatever. Just don't be something that you patently do not want to be.

And now is the time, not tomorrow. There is no time like the present. If you can't have what you want this very second the least you can do is start the journey now, this minute, while the inspiration is high. We all have the same amount of minutes, we all get the same 24 hours as Branson and Gates. It's just what we do with our time, how we invest it, that determines where our lives may lead.

So what I'm thinking is (and this is not molecular science) if we are dying and our allotted time is finite, why the hell aren't we doing all the things we want to do NOW? What's all this back-burner stuff? And why are we all waiting for the right time when we already know that the right time isn't going to show? The right time is the cheque that's permanently in the post, it never arrives. It's the girl who keeps us standing at the corner of the co-op looking like a spanner. No amount of clock watching will change the inevitable. She's stood us up.

We wait; the right time never arrives.

So I say stop waiting and meet providence half way. Start filling your life with the riches on offer so that when the reaper arrives, you'll have achieved so much, crammed your time so full that he'll fall asleep waiting for your life to flash before your eyes.

Act now or your time will elapse and you'll end up as a sepia-coloured relative that no one can put a name to in a dusty photo album.

Better to leave a biography as thick as a whale omelette than an epitaph.

'Joe Smith... hmmm. He didn't do much did he?'

Chapter 27

What do You Want to do?

I had a letter today from a friend. He was feeling a little sorry for himself (it's allowed – he is human) because he woke up one morning recently and realized why he'd been feeling so depressed for the last month or so. He was living without a purpose. Not that he'd never had a purpose, rather he'd had one and (somehow) lost it. It is easily done. My friend had once courted high aspirations; he was going to train in multi-disciplines and become a martial arts maverick, treading the world stage with the greats. He wanted (he told me) to be the best at something.

Being the funny guy that everyone knows I am I could easily have offered the hilarious advice I give most people who have lost something important. 'Why not look down the back of the settee?'

It is amazing what you can find if you move a few pillows and slide your fingers and wrist into that scary abyss. But from the gloomy tone of my friend's correspondence I figured that even a jokester as original as I might be wasting time with mirth when wisdom (and a quick solution) was being sought to the age-old problem: How do I find my purpose? How can I become the best at something?

In his email, my friend included a list of all the things that he had tried and not completed (this is part of the self-pity. 'Poor me, look at what a failure I am.' I've been here a hundred times myself), he talked about how well his partner was doing with her career, and how he was moving jobs and cities to support her (because he loved her) and also how pleased he was for her success. He also included a list of jobs he quite fancied doing, work that he thought might make 'a great career,' and perhaps one of them might even be the thing he could be the best at.

What he didn't include on his list was what he REALLY wanted to do.

I am not talking about what he thinks he should do or what others think he should do, or what is expected of him. I wasn't interested in what will earn him the most money or even what might offer the 'I've-made-it' status that so many people crave.

In the whole scope of things none of this is important. In colloquial speak, 'It's all bollocks.'

What I really wanted to know, and what I asked him (and what I now ask you) is this: WHAT DO YOU REALLY WANT TO DO? I mean REALLY.

Forget expectation. Forget income. Forget responsibilities. Forget what others want and expect and demand. Forget society, forget the government. Forget what you think and are told is impossible. What do you really want to do? If money and people were not an issue what is it that you would most like to spend your entire waking life doing? What is it that you love so much that time disappears when you do it? What is it that puts a light in your eyes at the mere mention of its name?

That (I told him, I tell you, I tell me) is what he should either be doing or at the very least making plans to do. No more and no less.

A job with great career prospects and great money has nothing whatsoever to do with following a dream. I have friends on six- and seven-figure incomes who hate the jobs that they do with a passion. They tell me that their life/job/family/commitments/mortgage keeps them imprisoned.

I tell them they are wrong. It is their ignorance that keeps them imprisoned.

I tell them that their right to choose differently will set them free.

Consider this: You spend two-thirds of your waking life at work. Do you really want to be bartering that much of your time just for a lifestyle? And anyway, who says you can't earn just as much money and enjoy just as good a lifestyle in a career that you love? I know millionaire plumbers, rich poets, wealthy martial artists.

If you are the best at what you do (and it is easier to be the best when you are passionate about what you do) the money will follow – it always follows passion.

It is at this point that people usually shake their heads and arch an eyebrow (as though I really don't get it) and say something like, 'I've got a mortgage to pay. I've got people relying on me. It is not that easy.'

To which I usually reply, 'I don't remember saying that it was easy. Only that it was possible.'

Of course it's difficult. If it was easy everybody would be doing it. And anyway, if everything came easy what would be the point? I have found that there is no flavour where there is no labour. What you work and strive for has a taste and texture that are only born from effort. I used to work full time as a martial-arts instructor. It was my job to train for a living. And I did train. When I did my 40 rounds on the bag after a five-mile run, a cup of tea was not just a cup of tea. It was a cup of tea! The taste, the texture, the smell, the feel – it was almost miraculous. Similarly, when I got my black belt in judo after some of the hardest training in my life, and certainly the most difficult grading I've ever done, I was a changed man. The lad that walked into the sports centre for the grading on Saturday morning was not the man who emerged on Saturday afternoon.

So hard is where it is at. It is the prerequisite to success. All those who walk around it, walk under it or over it, those that avoid 'hard' like it is a piece of shit on the floor, never get invited to the Emperor's banquet. They sit outside and (many of them) bitch about how the people inside got a lucky break, had it easy, knew someone on the inside (because, as we all know, 'it's who you know'). They wine because they feel overlooked, undervalued, hard-done-by or elbowed out. Or they claim that the person on the inside sold out. And the only reason they themselves didn't make it was because they maintained their integrity.

How noble.

And what a heap of horseshit.

This is the excuse offered by the people who just don't step up. How do I know? I have used the same excuse many times on my way to where I am now. And it wasn't until I buried that sickly heap of self-pity that I finally got on.

If you are good enough you make it. End of story. If you don't make it you look back into your self and take responsibility for that failing and either try again or quit bitching.

Back to my friend. He had lost his purpose. He wanted to find it again. He also wanted to be the best at something, though he was unsure of what that something might be. He was asking for my advice.

What I have learned from my 46-years of life is that anyone can be the best at anything if they are prepared to invest themselves in it (my book *Shapeshifter* has more on this process). To be the very best though, world class, global, I would say that four elements need to be in place.

1) First you need to acknowledge where you are right now. You need to do a brutal inventory of your level. This is important. I know many people (especially in the martial arts) who already think that they are world class and are constantly wondering why the world is not acknowledging them. I remember looking at one of my friends, a decent fighter with a whole heap of potential who wasn't taking that next step. It wasn't happening for him and I couldn't work out why. I said to Sharon, 'This guy has got so much potential. He could be world class. I can't work out what is holding him back.' She looked at him and said said to me, 'He thinks he is world class already.' She was so right. How was he ever going to try for the next level when he thought that he was already there?

So, give yourself an honest check-up. Don't inflate your ability and don't be self-depreciating. Where are you really? If you are not sure (and this is a hard one) ask the one person in your life who will tell you honestly. This needs to be someone that you trust, someone who is not afraid to tell you that you are great, but at the same time is not afraid to tell you that you are just not cutting it. A very famous drummer was approached by his teenage son. 'Dad,' he said, 'I am going to be a world-class drummer.' His dad looked at him and said, 'Then you'd better get busy because at the moment you just ain't doing the work, son.' The reply was harsh and to the point but this is the kind of honesty that you need if you want to be great. Once you have a realistic assessment of where you stand on the hierarchical ladder, you have to make sure the second element is in place.

2) You need an absolute passion for your subject matter. Finding a passion is often difficult for many people because while they want to do something great, they can't always work out what. From my experience, the 'what' in question is probably and usually something that you have always wanted to do since you were a child and would be prepared to do even if there was no money involved. If your purpose is not clear, a search is in order, usually the kind of search that goes in and not out. But if you are really serious about finding purpose don't worry, it'll find you when you are ready.

3) Once you have your purpose in place make sure that it is something that you personally believe you

can be the best at. If you are not sure that you can, maybe you feel too old, too young, too weak or too poor to make the top tier. Scan the book shops and Internet for proof to the opposite. Experience has told me that anyone can do anything. You don't have to look far for sterling examples of people who have achieved the most outrageous success, despite all the elements.

4) Ironically, if you want to aim high, what you do needs to be something that, eventually, you can earn a living from because to be the best at anything you need to work at it full time.

Once you have your four elements in place, it is about making that talk 'walk.' And walk. And walk. Many people talk about being the best at this and that. The martial artists talk about Lee or O'Neil, the guitarists talk Clapton or Hendrix, the screenwriters talk about Abbot or Webb Peoples but when you look closely that is all they do. They talk. And talking doesn't make a champion.

It is about reading it, writing it, watching it, hearing it, seeing it, feeling it, smelling it, talking it (but not too much talking). It is about taking it to bed with you and waking up with it on the tip of your tongue, eating it with your breakfast, supping it through the froth of your beer. It is about surrounding yourself with it and above all else it is about putting in the (thousands of hours of) practise (under escalating instruction) that is needed before the world stage offers you its boards to tread.

Beware. Aiming for pinnacles is uncomfortable. There is hardly any air up there in the higher echelons and you can suffer.

But that's good.

You will never be a great anything if you haven't suffered. Be worthy of the suffering and the struggle, so that when you arrive and people come to you for advise and complain about how hard their life is and how they are struggling, you can say, 'Hey, let tell you about struggle! I remember the time when… '

So, if like my friend you have lost your purpose, retrace your steps to a time when you were inspired, pick up the old scent and make a great adventure out of finding your purpose. If you want to be the best, stop talking and start doing. If this is a time of confusion for you, a time of struggle, get excited because that alone makes this is a great time. Confusion and struggle are the pre-cursers to major breakthroughs.

The universe is in dire need of adventurers and it is waiting for your contribution. Don't let it down.

Chapter 28

Who am I to be a Success?

I've had a few interesting conversations recently with people who really want to achieve some major goals in their lives but are plagued by a false belief that what it is they are aiming for is somehow not possible. 'And even if it is,' they say to me, 'who am I to be a success?'

I have lost count of the amount of times I have heard this comment (and even said the very same thing to myself in my darker moments). My heart goes out to all of those out there inflicted by this dreadful disease we call self-doubt. I know how debilitating it can be and I really do know how you feel.

It might help to know that you are not alone.

Most accomplished people feel this way at one time or another, often even after major successes. They just learn to override the negative voices in their heads and do the work anyway.

It took me a long time to believe in myself, but the more you push through the doubts and the more success you get behind you, the easier it gets. It helps to have some strong points of reference to fall back on. This entails getting a series of (even small) successes behind you to build on.

The great artist Escher was so full of insecurity and self-doubt that he would often feel an almost overpowering urge to stop a project, sometimes as soon as five minutes after starting. He learned to recognise this self-doubt as a pre-curser to all his great works. Because he recognised it he was able to step through it like a fog. He became massively successful not because he never felt doubt or fear, rather he was a success because he learned to ignore, and even use his fears as a fuel. Even the master Samurai on the battlefield is not without fear. His body still sweats and shivers with the anticipation of war, but he sets himself above his biology and steps into the arena not just despite his fear, but perhaps because of it.

It is inspiring to know that even the master feels the same pain and fear as you. But knowing is not enough – you have to 'do.'

Reading and listening will help you learn the process but the only true knowledge is earned knowledge. Loads of people have the facts. A plethora of folks can quote you book, line and verse on how to be the best 'this and that' on the planet, but information without experience is (what Shakespeare might have called) 'a giant's robe on a dwarfish thief.'

So when people ask me for lessons in becoming (for instance) a writer I always say the first lesson in writing is to write. The same as the first lesson of running is to run and the first lesson of fighting is to fight.

It is not the art of knowing, it is the art of doing.

So to be a writer just keep writing. Expect the fear, write anyway. Expect trepidation, set-backs, knock-backs, criticism, put-downs, depression, despair and the occasional failure. Once you have 'made it' expect the same again, when even your biggest fans call you all sorts of horrible names if your second book doesn't measure up (in their eyes) to your first or if you change style of try something new.

The critics lauded JD Salinger when he wrote the classic *Catcher in the Rye*. The very same critics savaged him when his second book was not to their liking. Salinger never published again.

Expect discomfort, it is the pre-requisite. All the gold is in the pain.

Remember this when you try to change in order to grow and the people who love you turn their love to hate because you go from writing articles to books, books to novels, novels to films or films to plays. They liked you as you were and where you were. Remember this when you try to change styles or systems or dogmas and the frightened and the wary warn you to 'leave well enough alone.' If you want to be anything – a writer, martial artist, tinker, tailor, soldier, sailor – more than the norm, I can tell you now that you have chosen a very difficult path. I applaud you for it because difficult in the game of life is categorically a green light and not a red. You have to be able to greet fear and doubt and (at times) utter despair along your chosen path and face these demons down.

Who are you to succeed?

Who the fuck are you not to?

You may deem great success an impossible thing, but it is not, nothing is. I have lost count of the number of people who told me that I was kidding myself when I said I wanted to become a top martial artist and when I said I was going to write books and films. Close friends. Even people that I loved scoffed at me. That is why I was so elated at the BAFTAs because it proved to all of them (and to myself) that I (and they) can do anything.

Everything you want resides just behind that membrane of fear you are feeling right now. To get the gold, you have to get past the fear.

Chapter 29

You Are What You Ingest

Have you noticed how many programmes there are on the telly these days about healthy eating? Everything from *Jamie's Dinners* to Dr Gillian McKeith's *You Are What You Eat*. I love it. I do. I think it's long overdue. We've all known (or at least we have always been told) that the food we take in determines the performance we give out. We also know (or should anyway) that the leading cause of death (heart disease) finds its way in through bad eating habits. If this is the case – and the evidence for it is compelling – why do so many people still continue to eat a diet of poison ivy and expect rose-petal health? Why (as the old adage goes) do we do what we do when we know what we know?

This is a question I am going to leave you to ponder on. Mostly because the answer is as obvious as your nose. It is not physical food that I find completely intriguing, it is cerebral food.

I have spent most of my life reviewing and studying diet in my search for self-improvement (if not enlightenment) and through years of trial and error I managed to get my diet pretty tight. I have to say that I did feel a lot better for it. Energy was up, health was up, performance improved, mood found a steady and happy homeostasis. But even with my food in place there was still something missing. There was still a piece of the jigsaw lost. It was at this point I had a great realisation. You can get your diet as tight as you like and it still will not bring you optimum results if your thoughts aren't right. Don't get me wrong. Healthy eating improves thinking no end, but to take your thoughts to an Olympic level you need to start watching your cerebral diet. Thinking comes through and from the brain, and the brain has several forms of nutrition, the mainstay being information. This is not a statement of metaphor. Information is a literal food for the brain, it relies upon it for growth, and whether that growth is healthy or not depends entirely upon the quality of your information ingested. In fact every piece of information that you absorb becomes chemicals in your body. Watch a porn flick or a violent movie and the body will explode with a cocktail of stress hormones looking for a fuck or a fight, and if it doesn't get one (of either) those same hormones will quickly turn rogue. Watch a movie about Gandhi or have a conversation about the global power of love with Mother Teresa and you'll be filled with endorphins and probably want to save a small village in India or tell someone close that you love them.

Your daily diet of cerebral grub consists of what you watch on TV, listen to on the radio, read, who you talk to (this includes talking to yourself), hang out with, marry, admire and mimic. Stand with gangsters and you'll get the violent high-octane kick of adrenalin that makes you want to set up a business in the dark arts. Have an afternoon with Deepak Chopra and you'll probably want to study metaphysics and manifest your dreams out of mid-air. Spend the evening having it large with the pub cynics and you may doubt the very existence of good by the end of the evening. Have an afternoon with BJJ maverick John B. Will and you'll be inspired to traverse the globe – like he has – in search of great martial mentors. Even your environment feeds your brain. If you are in a shitty part of the city under constant threat of attack don't believe for even a second that it will not feed your brain. But is this the kind of nutrition that you want?

I am telling you all this but you know it already. If you have been around for even two decades you will have experienced enough to know that influences influence. And if they are strong influences they influence strongly.

Here's the good news and the bad news. Good news first. Like physical diet, cerebral diet can be changed. Your environment and influences, what you watch and read and who you talk to can be changed in the beat of a healthy heart.

If you have the foresight and the courage.

Bad news. Like physical diet, cerebral nutrition needs to be consistent. The good results only last as long as the good information. It needs to be topped-up daily until it is habit. One bad day on a food binge can throw you into a state of nutritional crisis (your organs are high priority, you only get the one set). Equally, one bad night of poor choice company could throw you in jail or worse. The mortuary slab has no respect for prior good behaviour.

I have seen many a good soul made obese simply because of greedy and poor-choice eating. I have seen many a good soul turn gangrenous simply because of poor-choice friends.

So I say be very fussy about what you ingest. Everything that goes in will come out in a similar fashion. If you don't want to see the replay of bad health for the rest of your life, get your bollocks on the table and make the changes. Stop pretending that what you eat and who you sit with doesn't affect the very foundation of who you are.

You are what you ingest. So ingest what you want to be.

The Elephant and The Twig
The Art of Positive Thinking

Geoff Thompson

£9.99 P/b

ISBN: 1-84024-264-7
ISBN 13: 978-1-84024-264-5

In India, young elephants are trained in obedience by being tied to an immovable object like a tree. No matter how hard the baby elephant pulls it cannot break free, and eventually, after trying to break away and being thwarted time and again, it believes that it cannot escape, no matter what it does. Ultimately, a fully-grown adult weighing several tons can be tied to a twig and won't even try to escape.

Do you ever feel that you are tied to an immovable object and can't break free? That you couldn't possibly give that presentation, that you would never be able to go it alone in business, or that you have to remain stuck in a social and lifestyle rut as there is no other alternative? This book argues that what ties you down and prevents you from realising your potential is only a 'twig'. Geoff guides you through the process of breaking the negative thinking that binds us and reveals the '14 Golden Rules to Success and Happiness'.

TALES FROM SHAKESPEARE

" O how I love you! " said the Fairy Queen

(SEE PAGE 76)

TALES FROM
SHAKESPEARE

FROM THE COLLECTION BY
CHARLES AND MARY LAMB

ILLUSTRATED BY WILLIAM STOBBS

BLACKIE

LONDON AND GLASGOW

BLACKIE & SON LIMITED
5 FITZHARDINGE STREET
PORTMAN SQUARE
LONDON · W.I

BISHOPBRIGGS, GLASGOW

BLACKIE & SON
(INDIA) LIMITED
103-5 FORT STREET
BOMBAY

PRINTED IN GREAT BRITAIN BY BLACKIE & SON LIMITED · GLASGOW

Contents

—◦⧸—⧹◦❀⁝⁞⧸⧹❀◦❧—❦◦—

As You Like It

DURING THE TIME that France was divided into provinces (or dukedoms as they were called) there reigned in one of these provinces a usurper, who had deposed and banished his elder brother, the lawful duke.

The duke, who was thus driven from his dominions, retired with a few faithful followers to the forest of Arden. Here the good duke lived with his loving friends, who had put themselves into exile of their own accord for his sake, while their lands and wealth enriched the false usurper. Custom soon made the life of careless ease they led here more sweet to them than the pomp and uneasy splendour of a life at court.

There they lived like the old Robin Hood of England, and to this forest many noble youths resorted from the court, and did pass the time carelessly, as they did who lived in the golden age. In the summer they lay along under the fine shade of the large forest trees, marking the playful sports of the wild deer. So fond were they of these poor dappled fools, who seemed to be the native inhabitants of the forest, that it grieved them to be forced to kill them to supply themselves with venison for their food.

When the cold winds of winter made the duke feel the change of his adverse fortune, he would endure it patiently, and say, 'These chilling winds which blow upon my body are true counsellors. They do not flatter, but represent truly to me my condition. Though they bite sharply, their tooth is nothing like so keen as that of unkindness or unthankfulness. I find that, howsoever men speak against adversity, yet some sweet uses are to be got from it; like the jewel, precious for medicine, which is taken from the head of the venomous and despised toad.'

In this manner did the patient duke draw a useful lesson from everything that he saw, and by the help of this turn of mind, in that life of his, remote from public haunts, he could find tongues in trees, books in the running brooks, sermons in stones, and good in everything.

The banished duke had an only daughter, named Rosalind, whom the usurper, Duke Frederick, when he banished her father, still kept in his court as a companion for his own daughter Celia. A great friendship existed between these ladies, which the disagreement between their fathers did not in the least break; Celia striving by every kindness in her power to make amends to Rosalind for the wrong done by her own father in deposing the father of Rosalind. Whenever the thoughts of her father's banishment, and her need to depend so much on the false usurper, made Rosalind sad, Celia's whole care was to comfort and console her.

One day, when Celia was talking in her usual kind manner to Rosalind, saying, 'I pray you, Rosalind, my sweet cousin, be merry,' a messenger entered from the duke. He came to tell them that if they wished to see a wrestling match, which was just going to begin, they must come at once to the court before the palace. Celia, thinking it would amuse Rosalind, agreed to go and see it.

In those times wrestling, which is only practised now by country clowns, was a favourite sport even in the courts of princes, and before fair ladies and princesses. To this wrestling match, therefore, Celia and Rosalind went. They found that it was likely to be a very sorrowful sight, for a large and powerful man, who had long been practised in the art of wrestling, and had slain many men in contests of this kind, was just going to wrestle with a very young man. The latter, from his youth and want of practice in the art, the beholders all thought would certainly be killed.

When the duke saw Celia and Rosalind, he said, 'How now, daughter and niece, have you crept hither to see the wrestling? You will take little delight in it; there is such odds in the men. In pity to this young man, I would wish to persuade him from wrestling. Speak to him, ladies, and see if you can move him.'

The ladies were well pleased to do this, and first Celia entreated the young stranger that he would not make the attempt. Then Rosalind spoke so kindly to him, and with such feeling thoughtfulness for the danger he was about to undergo, that, instead of being persuaded by her gentle words to give up his purpose, all his thoughts were bent on displaying his courage before this lovely lady's eyes.

He refused the request of Celia and Rosalind in such graceful and modest words, that they felt still more concern for him. He ended his refusal by saying, 'I am sorry to deny such fair and excellent ladies anything. But let your fair eyes and gentle wishes go with me to my trial, wherein, if I be conquered, there is one shamed that was never gracious; if I am killed, there is one dead, that is willing to die. I shall do my friends no wrong, for I have none to lament me; the world no injury, for in it I have nothing; for I only fill up a place in the world which may be better supplied when I have made it empty.'

*   *   *

Now the wrestling match began. Celia wished the young stranger might not be hurt, but Rosalind felt most for him. The friendless state which he said he was in, and that he wished to die, made Rosalind think that he was, like herself, in misfortune. She pitied him so much, and took so deep an interest in his danger while he was wrestling, that she might almost be said at that moment to have fallen in love with him.

The kindness shown this unknown youth by these fair and noble ladies, gave him courage and strength, so that he performed wonders, and in the end completely conquered his rival, who was so much hurt that for a while he was unable to speak or move.

The Duke Frederick was much pleased with the courage and skill shown by this young stranger, and desired to know what was his name and who were his parents, meaning to take him under his care.

The stranger said his name was Orlando, and

that he was the youngest son of Sir Rowland de Bois.

Sir Rowland de Bois, the father of Orlando, had been dead some years. But when he was living he had been a true subject and dear friend of the banished duke. Therefore, when Frederick heard Orlando was the son of his banished brother's friend, all his liking for this brave young man was changed into displeasure, and he left the place in very ill humour. Hating to hear the very name of any of his brother's friends, and yet still admiring the valour of the youth, he said as he went out that he wished Orlando had been the son of any other man.

Rosalind was delighted to hear that her new favourite was the son of her father's old friend, and she said to Celia, 'My father loved Sir Rowland de Bois, and if I had known this young man was his son, I would have added tears to my entreaties before he should have ventured.'

The ladies then went up to him, and, seeing him abashed by the sudden displeasure shown by the duke, they spoke kind and encouraging words to him. Rosalind, when they were going away, turned back to speak some more civil things to the brave young son of her father's old friend; and, taking a chain from off her neck, she said, 'Gentleman, wear this for me. I am out of suits with fortune, or I would give you a more valuable present.'

When the ladies were alone, Rosalind's talk being still of Orlando, Celia began to perceive her cousin had fallen in love with the handsome young wrestler, and she said to Rosalind, 'Is it possible you should fall in love so suddenly?' Rosalind replied, 'The duke, my father, loved his father dearly.' 'But,' said Celia, 'does it therefore follow that you should love his son dearly? for then I ought to hate him, for my father hated his father; yet I do not hate Orlando.'

Frederick being enraged at the sight of Sir Rowland de Bois' son, which reminded him of the many friends the banished duke had among the nobles, and having been for some time displeased with his niece, because the people praised her for her virtues, and pitied her for her good father's sake, his malice suddenly broke out against her. While Celia and Rosalind were talking of Orlando, Frederick entered the room, and with looks of anger ordered Rosalind at once to leave the palace and follow her father into banishment, telling Celia, who in vain pleaded for her, that he had only suffered Rosalind to stay upon her account.

'I did not then,' said Celia, 'entreat you to let her stay, for I was too young at that time to value her; but now that I know her worth, and that we so long have slept together, risen at the same instant, learned, played, and eaten together, I cannot live out of her company.'

Frederick replied, 'She is too subtle for you; her smoothness, her very silence and her patience speak to the people, and they pity her. You are a fool to plead for her, for you will seem more bright and virtuous when she is gone; therefore open not your lips in her favour, for the doom which I have passed upon her cannot be recalled.'

When Celia found she could not prevail upon her father to let Rosalind remain with her, she generously resolved to go with her. Leaving her father's palace that night, she went along with her friend to seek Rosalind's father, the banished duke, in the forest of Arden.

*　　*　　*

Before they set out, Celia considered that it would be unsafe for two young ladies to travel in the rich clothes they then wore. She therefore proposed that they should disguise their rank by dressing themselves like country maids. Rosalind said it would protect them still more if one of them was to be dressed like a man. So it was quickly agreed on between them, that as Rosalind was the taller, she should wear the dress of a young countryman, and Celia should be dressed like a country lass, and that they should say they were brother and sister. Rosalind said she would be called Ganymede, and Celia chose the name of Aliena.

In this disguise, and taking their money and jewels to pay their expenses, these fair princesses set out on their long travel, for the forest of Arden was a long way off, beyond the duke's dominions.

The lady Rosalind (or Ganymede, as she must now be called) with her manly garb seemed to have put on a manly courage. The faithful friendship Celia had shown in going with Rosalind so many weary miles made the new brother, in recompense for this true love, exert a cheerful spirit, as if he were indeed Ganymede, the rustic and stout-hearted brother of the gentle village maiden, Aliena.

When at last they came to the forest of Arden, they no longer found the good inns they had met with on the road, and being in want of food and rest, Ganymede, who had so merrily cheered his sister with pleasant speeches and happy remarks all the way, now owned to Aliena that he was so weary he could find in his heart to disgrace his man's apparel and cry like a woman. Aliena declared she could go no farther, and then again Ganymede tried to recollect that it was a man's duty to comfort and console a woman as the weaker vessel, and, to seem full of courage to his new sister, he said, 'Come, have a good heart, my sister Aliena; we are now at the end of our travel in the forest of Arden.'

But pretended manliness and forced courage would no longer support them, for though they were in the forest of Arden they knew not where to find the duke, and here the travel of these weary ladies might have come to a sad end, for they might have lost themselves and have perished for want of food. But as they were sitting on the grass, almost dying with weariness and hopeless of any relief, a countryman chanced to pass that way. Ganymede once more tried to speak with a manly boldness, saying, 'Shepherd, if love or gold can in this desert place procure us entertainment, I pray you bring us where we may rest ourselves, for this young maid, my sister, is much worn-out with travelling, and faints for want of food.'

The man replied that he was only servant to a shepherd, and that his master's house was just going to be sold, and therefore they would find but poor entertainment, but that if they would go with him they should be welcome to what there was. They followed the man, the near prospect of relief giving them fresh strength, and bought the house and sheep of the shepherd, and took the man who conducted them to the shepherd's house to wait on them. Being by this means so fortunately provided with a neat cottage, and well supplied with food, they agreed to stay here till they could learn in what part of the forest the duke dwelt.

When they were rested, after the weariness of their journey, they began to like their new way of life, and almost fancied themselves the shepherd and shepherdess they pretended to be. Yet sometimes Ganymede remembered he had once been the same Lady Rosalind who had so dearly loved the brave Orlando, because he was the son of old Sir Rowland, her father's friend, and though Ganymede thought that Orlando was many miles distant, even so many weary miles as they had travelled, yet it soon appeared that Orlando was also in the forest of Arden, and in this manner this strange event came to pass.

Orlando was the youngest son of Sir Rowland de Bois, who, when he died, left him (Orlando being then very young) to the care of his eldest brother Oliver, charging Oliver, on his blessing, to give his brother a good education, and provide for him as became their ancient house. Oliver proved an unworthy brother, and, disregarding the commands of his dying father, he never put his brother to school, but kept him at home untaught and entirely neglected. But in his nature and in the noble qualities of his mind Orlando so much resembled his excellent father that, without any advantages of education, he seemed like a youth who had been bred with the utmost care. Oliver so envied the fine person and gentle manners of his untutored brother, that at last he wished to destroy him. To effect this he set on people to persuade him to wrestle with the famous wrestler, who, as has been before related, had killed so many men. Now it was this cruel brother's neglect of him which made Orlando say he wished to die, being so friendless.

When, contrary to the wicked hopes he had formed, his brother proved victorious, his envy and wickedness knew no bounds, and he swore he would burn the chamber where Orlando slept. He was overheard making this vow by one who had been an old and faithful friend to their father, and who loved Orlando because he resembled Sir Rowland. This old man went out to meet him when he returned from the duke's palace, and when he saw Orlando, the peril his dear young master was in made him break out in these words: 'O, my gentle master, my sweet master; O, you memory of old Sir Rowland! why are you virtuous, why are you gentle, strong, and brave, and why would you be so fond of overcoming the famous wrestler? Your praise is come too swiftly home before you.'

Orlando, wondering what all this meant, asked him what was the matter. Then the old man told him how his wicked brother, envying the love all the people bore him, and now hearing the fame he had gained by his victory in the duke's palace, intended to destroy him by setting fire to his chamber that night; and advised him to escape the danger he was in by instant flight. Knowing Orlando had no money, Adam (for that was the good old man's name) had brought out with him his own little hoard, and he said, 'I have five hundred crowns, the thrifty hire I saved under your father, and laid by to be provision for me when my old limbs should become unfit for service; take that, and He that doth the ravens feed be comfort to my age! Here is the gold; all this I give to you; let me be your servant; though I look old, I will do the service of a younger man in all your business and needs.'

'O good old man!' said Orlando, 'how well appears in you the constant service of the old world! You are not for the fashion of these times. We will go along together, and before your youthful wages are spent, I shall light upon some means for both our support.'

*   *   *

Together, then, this faithful servant and his loved master set out. Orlando and Adam travelled on uncertain what course to follow, till they came to the forest of Arden, and there they found themselves in the same distress for want of food that Ganymede and Aliena had been. They wandered on, seeking some human dwelling, till they were almost spent with hunger and weariness.

Adam at last said, 'O my dear master, I die for want of food, I can go no farther!' He then laid himself down, thinking to make that place his grave, and bade his dear master farewell. Orlando, seeing him in this weak state, took his old servant up in his arms, and carried him under the shelter of some pleasant trees; and he said to him, 'Cheerily, old Adam, rest your weary limbs here a while, and do not talk of dying!'

Orlando then searched about to find some food, and he happened to arrive at that part of the forest where the duke was. He and his friends were just going to eat their dinner, this royal duke being seated on the grass under no other canopy than the shady cover of some large trees.

Orlando, whom hunger had made very bold, drew his sword, intending to take their meat by force, and said, 'Forbear, and eat no more; I must have your food!' The duke asked him if distress had made him so bold, or if he were a rude despiser of good manners. On this Orlando said he was dying with hunger, and then the duke told him he was welcome to sit down and eat with them.

Orlando, hearing him speak so gently, put up his sword, and blushed with shame at the rude manner in which he had demanded their food. 'Pardon me, I pray you,' said he; 'I thought that all things had been savage here, and therefore I put on the appearance of stern command. But whatever men you are that in this desert, under the shade of sad boughs, lose and neglect the creeping hours of time; if ever you have looked on better days; if ever you have been where bells have rung to church; if you have ever sat at any good man's feast; if ever from your eyelids you have wiped a tear, and know what it is to pity or be pitied, may gentle speeches now move you to do me human courtesy!'

The duke replied, 'True it is that we are men (as you say) who have seen better days, and though we have now our dwelling in this wild forest, we have lived in towns and cities, and have with holy bell been rung to church, have sat at good men's feasts, and from our eyes have wiped the drops which sacred pity has called forth. Therefore sit you down, and take of our refreshment as much as will minister to your wants.'

'There is a poor old man,' answered Orlando, 'who has limped after me many a weary step in pure love, oppressed at once with two sad things, age and hunger; till he be satisfied I must not touch a bit.'

'Go, find him out, and bring him hither,' said the duke; 'we will forbear to eat till you return.' Then Orlando went like a doe to find its fawn and give it food, and presently returned bringing Adam in his arms. The duke said, 'Set down your burden; you are both welcome.' They fed the old man and cheered his heart, and he revived, and recovered his health and strength again.

The duke enquired who Orlando was, and when he found that he was the son of his old friend, Sir Rowland de Bois, he took him under his care, and Orlando and his old servant lived with the duke in the forest.

Orlando arrived in the forest not many days after Ganymede and Aliena came there and (as has been before related) bought the shepherd's cottage.

* * *

Ganymede and Aliena were strangely surprised
to find the name of Rosalind carved on the trees,
and love sonnets fastened to them, all addressed

to Rosalind. While they were wondering how this could be, they met Orlando, and they saw the chain which Rosalind had given him about his neck.

Orlando little thought that Ganymede was the fair princess Rosalind, who, by her noble favour, had so won his heart that he passed his whole time in carving her name upon the trees, and writing sonnets in praise of her beauty. Being much pleased with the graceful air of this pretty shepherd youth, he talked with him. He thought he saw a likeness in Ganymede to his beloved Rosalind, but that he had none of the dignified bearing of that noble lady. For Ganymede put on the forward manners often seen in youths when they are between boys and men, and with much archness and humour talked to Orlando of a certain lover, 'who', said he, 'haunts our forest, and spoils our young trees with carving Rosalind upon their barks; and he hangs odes upon hawthorns, and sonnets on brambles, all praising this same Rosalind. If I could find this lover, I would give him some good advice that would soon cure him of his love.'

Orlando confessed that he was the fond lover of whom he spoke, and asked Ganymede to give him the good advice he talked of. The cure Ganymede proposed, and the advice he gave him, was that Orlando should come every day to the cottage where he and his sister Aliena dwelt. 'And then,' said Ganymede, 'I will pretend myself to be Rosalind, and you shall pretend to court me in the same manner as you would do if I was Rosalind, and then I will imitate the ways of ladies to their lovers, till I make you ashamed of your love; and this is the way I propose to cure you.'

Orlando had no great faith in the cure, yet he agreed to come every day to Ganymede's cottage and pretend a playful courtship. Every day Orlando visited Ganymede and Aliena, and Orlando called the shepherd Ganymede his Rosalind, and every day talked over all the fine and flattering words, which young men delight to use when they court their mistresses. It does not appear, however, that Ganymede made any progress in curing Orlando of his love for Rosalind.

Though Orlando thought all this but a sportive play (not dreaming that Ganymede was his very Rosalind), yet the chance it gave him of saying all the fond things he had in his heart pleased his fancy almost as well as it did Ganymede's, who enjoyed the secret jest in knowing these fine love speeches were addressed to the right person.

In this manner many days passed pleasantly on with these young people. The good-natured Aliena, seeing it made Ganymede happy, let him have his own way, and was amused at the mock courtship, and did not care to remind Ganymede that the Lady Rosalind had not yet made herself known to the duke her father, whose place of resort in the forest they had learnt from Orlando.

Ganymede met the duke one day, and had some talk with him, and the duke asked who were his parents. Ganymede answered that he had as good parents as the duke had, which made him smile, for he did not suspect the pretty shepherd boy was the son of a prince. Then seeing the duke look well and happy, Ganymede was content to put off explaining further for a few days longer.

*   *   *

One morning, as Orlando was going to visit Ganymede, he saw a man lying asleep on the ground, and a large green snake had twisted itself about his neck. The snake, seeing Orlando approach, glided away among the bushes. Orlando went nearer, and then he discovered a lioness lying couching, with her head on the ground, with a cat-like watch, waiting till the sleeping man awaked (for it is said that lions will prey on nothing that is dead or sleeping).

It seemed as if Orlando was sent by Providence to free the man from the danger of the snake and lioness. When Orlando looked in the man's face, he perceived that the sleeper, who was exposed to this double peril, was his own brother Oliver, who had so cruelly used him, and had threatened to destroy him by fire, and he was almost tempted to leave him a prey to the hungry lioness. But brotherly affection and the gentleness of his nature soon overcame his first anger against his brother, and he drew his sword and attacked the lioness, and slew her, and thus preserved his brother's life both from the venomous snake and from the furious lioness. Before Orlando could conquer the lioness, she had torn one of his arms with her sharp claws.

While Orlando was engaged with the lioness, Oliver awaked, and seeing that his brother Orlando, whom he had so cruelly treated, was saving him from the fury of a wild beast at the risk of his own life, shame and grief at once seized him, and he was sorry for his unworthy conduct, and besought with many tears his brother's pardon for the injuries he had done him. Orlando rejoiced to see him so sorry, and readily forgave him. They embraced each other, and from that hour Oliver loved Orlando with a true brotherly love, though he had come to the forest bent on killing him.

The wound in Orlando's arm having bled very much, he found himself too weak to go to visit Ganymede, and therefore he desired his brother to go and tell Ganymede, 'whom,' said Orlando, 'I in sport do call my Rosalind,' the accident which had befallen him.

Thither then Oliver went, and told to Ganymede and Aliena how Orlando had saved his life. When he had finished the story of Orlando's bravery, and his own escape, he owned to them that he was Orlando's brother, who had so cruelly used him. Then he told them that they had now become friends.

The sincere sorrow that Oliver expressed for his offences made such a lively impression on the kind heart of Aliena, that she instantly fell in love with him. Oliver, observing how much she pitied the distress he told her he felt for his fault, he as suddenly fell in love with her. But while love was thus stealing into the hearts of Aliena and Oliver, he was no less busy with Ganymede, who, hearing of the danger Orlando had been in, and that he was wounded by the lioness, fainted. When he recovered, he pretended that he had swooned in the character of Rosalind, and Ganymede said to Oliver, 'Tell your brother Orlando how well I pretended to swoon.'

But Oliver saw by the paleness of his face that he did really faint, and, much wondering at the weakness of the young man, he said, 'Well, if you did pretend, take a good heart, and pretend to be a man.' 'So I do,' replied Ganymede truly, 'but I should have been a woman by right.'

Oliver made this visit a very long one, and when at last he returned to his brother, he had much news to tell him. For, besides the account of Ganymede's fainting at the hearing that Orlando was wounded, Oliver told him how he had fallen in love with the fair shepherdess, Aliena, and that she had lent a favourable ear to his suit, even in this their first interview. He talked to his brother, as of a thing almost settled, that he should marry Aliena, saying that he so well loved her that he would live here as a shepherd, and settle his estate and house at home upon Orlando.

'You have my consent,' said Orlando. 'Let your wedding be tomorrow, and I will invite the duke and his friends. Go and persuade your shepherdess to agree to this: she is now alone, for look, here comes her brother.' Oliver went to Aliena; and Ganymede, whom Orlando had perceived approaching, came to enquire after the health of his wounded friend.

*　　*　　*

When Orlando and Ganymede began to talk over the sudden love which had taken place between Oliver and Aliena, Orlando said he had advised his brother to persuade his fair shepherdess to be married on the morrow, and then he added how much he could wish to be married on the same day to his Rosalind.

Ganymede, who well approved of this arrangement, said, that if Orlando really loved Rosalind as well as he professed to do, he should have his wish. On the morrow he would engage to make Rosalind appear in her own person, and also that Rosalind should be willing to marry Orlando.

This seemingly wonderful event, which, as Ganymede was the Lady Rosalind, he could so easily perform, he pretended he would bring to pass by the aid of magic, which he said he had learnt of an uncle who was a famous magician.

The fond lover Orlando, half-believing and half-doubting what he heard, asked Ganymede if he spoke in sober meaning. 'By my life I do,' said Ganymede; 'therefore put on your best clothes, and bid the duke and your friends to your wedding; for if you desire to be married to-morrow to Rosalind, she shall be here.'

The next morning, Oliver having obtained the consent of Aliena, they came into the presence of the duke, and with them also came Orlando.

They being all assembled to celebrate this double marriage, and as yet only one of the brides appearing, there was much of wonder, but they mostly thought that Ganymede was making a jest of Orlando.

The duke, hearing that it was his own daughter that was to be brought in this strange way, asked Orlando if he believed the shepherd boy could really do what he had promised. While Orlando was answering that he knew not what to think, Ganymede entered and asked the duke, if he brought his daughter, whether he would consent to her marriage with Orlando. 'That I would,' said the duke, 'if I had kingdoms to give with her.' Ganymede then said to Orlando, 'And you say you will marry her if I bring her here?' 'That I would,' said Orlando, 'if I were king of many kingdoms.'

Ganymede and Aliena then went out together, and Ganymede throwing off his male attire and being once more dressed in woman's clothing, quickly became Rosalind without the power of magic. Aliena, changing her country garb for her own rich clothes, was with as little trouble transformed into the Lady Celia.

While they were gone, the duke said to Orlando that he thought the shepherd Ganymede was very like his daughter Rosalind; and Orlando said he also had observed the likeness.

They had no time to wonder how all this would end, for Rosalind and Celia in their own clothes entered. No longer pretending that it was by the power of magic that she came there, Rosalind threw herself on her knees before her father and begged his blessing. It seemed so wonderful to all present that she should so suddenly appear, that it might well have passed for magic. But Rosalind would no longer trifle with her father, but told him the story of her banishment, and of her dwelling in the forest as a shepherd boy, her cousin Celia passing as her sister.

The duke confirmed the consent he had already given to the marriage. Orlando and Rosalind, Oliver and Celia, were married at the same time. And though their wedding could not be celebrated in this wild forest with any of the parade or splendour usual on such occasions, yet a happier wedding-day was never passed. While they were eating their venison under the cool shade of the trees, as if nothing should be wanting to complete the happiness of this good duke and the true lovers, an unexpected messenger arrived to tell the duke the joyful news that his dukedom was restored to him.

The usurper, enraged at the flight of his daughter Celia, and hearing that every day men of great worth resorted to the forest of Arden to join the lawful duke in his exile, much envying that his brother should be so highly respected in his adversity, put himself at the head of a large force and advanced to the forest, intending to seize his brother and put him, with all his faithful followers, to the sword. But by a wonderful Providence, this bad brother was converted from his evil intention. For, just as he entered the skirts of the wild forest, he was met by an old religious man, a hermit, with whom he had much talk, and who in the end completely turned his heart from his wicked purpose. Thenceforward he became truly sorry, and resolved, giving up his unjust dominion, to spend the remainder of his days in a religious house. The first act of his new sorrow was to send a messenger to his brother (as has been related) to offer to restore to him his dukedom, which he had usurped so long, and with it the lands and wealth of his friends, the faithful followers of his adversity.

This joyful news, as unexpected as it was

welcome, came at the right time to heighten the rejoicings at the wedding of the princesses. Celia complimented her cousin on this good fortune which had happened to the duke, Rosalind's father, and wished her joy very sincerely, though she herself was no longer heir to the dukedom, but by this restoration which her father had made Rosalind was now the heir. So completely was the love of these two cousins unmixed with anything of envy.

The duke had now a chance of rewarding those true friends who had stayed with him in his banishment, and these worthy followers, though they had patiently shared his adverse fortune, were very well pleased to return in peace and prosperity to the palace of their lawful duke.

—⋅✤⋅✤⋅✤⋅⋅✤⋅✤⋅✤⋅—

Much Ado About Nothing

THERE LIVED IN THE PALACE at Messina two
ladies, whose names were Hero and Beatrice.
Hero was the daughter, and Beatrice the niece,
of Leonato the Governor of Messina.

Beatrice was of a lively temper, and loved to
divert her cousin Hero, who was of a more serious
disposition, with her sprightly sallies. Whatever
was going forward was sure to make matter of
mirth for the light-hearted Beatrice.

At the time the history of these ladies com-
mences, some young men of high rank in the
army, as they were passing through Messina on
their return from a war that was just ended, in
which they had distinguished themselves by their
great bravery, came to visit Leonato. Among
these were Don Pedro, the Prince of Arragon,
and his friend Claudio, who was a lord of Florence.
With them came the wild and witty Benedick, and
he was a lord of Padua.

These strangers had been at Messina before,

and the hospitable governor introduced them to his daughter and his niece as their old friends and acquaintances.

Benedick, the moment he entered the room, began a lively conversation with Leonato and the prince. Beatrice, who liked not to be left out of any discourse, interrupted Benedick with saying, 'I wonder that you will still be talking, Signor Benedick; nobody marks you.' Benedick was just such another rattle-brain as Beatrice, yet he was not pleased at this free salutation. He thought it did not become a well-bred lady to be so flippant with her tongue; and he remembered, when he was last at Messina, that Beatrice used to select him to make her merry jests upon. As there is no one who so little likes to be made a jest of as those who are apt to take the same liberty themselves, so it was with Benedick and Beatrice. These two sharp wits never met in former times but a perfect war of raillery was kept up between them, and they always parted mutually displeased with each other. Therefore when Beatrice stopped him in the middle of his discourse with telling him nobody marked what he was saying, Benedick, affecting not to have observed before that she was present, said, 'What, my dear Lady Disdain, are you yet living?'

Now war broke out afresh between them, and

a long jangling argument ensued, during which Beatrice, although she knew he had so well approved his valour in the late war, said that she could eat all that he had killed there; and observing the prince take delight in Benedick's conversation, she called him 'the prince's jester'. This sarcasm sank deeper into the mind of Benedick than all Beatrice had said before. The hint she gave him that he was a coward, by saying she would eat all he had killed, he did not regard, knowing himself to be a brave man; but there is nothing that great wits dread so much as the imputation of buffoonery, because the charge comes sometimes a little too near the truth; therefore Benedick perfectly hated Beatrice when she called him 'the prince's jester'.

The modest Lady Hero was silent before the noble guests, and while Claudio was attentively observing the improvement which time had made in her beauty, and was contemplating the exquisite graces of her fine figure (for she was an admirable young lady), the prince was highly amused with listening to the humorous dialogue between Benedick and Beatrice, and he said in a whisper to Leonato, 'This is a pleasant-spirited young lady. She were an excellent wife for Benedick.' Leonato replied to this suggestion, 'O my lord, my lord, if they were but a week married, they would talk themselves mad.' But though Leonato thought they would make a quarrelsome pair, the prince did not give up the idea of matching these two keen wits together.

When the prince returned with Claudio from the palace, he found that the marriage he had devised between Benedick and Beatrice was not the only one projected in that good company, for Claudio spoke in such terms of Hero as made the prince guess at what was passing in his heart; and he liked it well, and he said to Claudio, 'Do you affect Hero?'

To this question Claudio replied, 'O my lord, when I was last at Messina I looked upon her with a soldier's eye that liked, but had no leisure for loving; but now, in this happy time of peace, thoughts of war have left their places vacant in my mind, and in their room come thronging soft and delicate thoughts, all prompting me how fair young Hero is, reminding me that I liked her before I went to the wars.'

Claudio's confession of his love for Hero so wrought upon the prince that he lost no time in asking the consent of Leonato to accept of Claudio for a son-in-law. Leonato agreed to this proposal, and the prince found no great difficulty in persuading the gentle Hero herself to listen to the suit of the noble Claudio, who was a lord of rare endowments, and highly accomplished; and Claudio, assisted by his kind prince, soon prevailed upon Leonato to fix an early day for the celebration of his marriage with Hero.

Claudio was to wait but a few days before he was to be married to his fair lady. Yet he complained of the interval being tedious, as indeed most young men are impatient when they are waiting for the accomplishment of any event they have set their hearts upon. The prince, therefore, to make the time seem short to him, proposed, as a kind of merry pastime, that they should invent some artful scheme to make Benedick and Beatrice fall in love with each other. Claudio entered with great satisfaction into this whim of the prince, and Leonato promised them his assistance, and even Hero said she would do any modest office to help her cousin to a good husband.

The device the prince invented was, that the gentlemen should make Benedick believe that Beatrice was in love with him, and that Hero should make Beatrice believe that Benedick was in love with her.

The prince, Leonato, and Claudio began their operations first. Watching an opportunity when Benedick was quietly seated reading in an arbour, the prince and his assistants took their station among the trees behind the arbour, so near that Benedick could not choose but hear all they said. After some careless talk, the prince said, 'Come hither, Leonato. What was it you told me the other day—that your niece Beatrice was in love with Signor Benedick? I did never think that lady would have loved any man.'

'No, nor I either, my lord,' answered Leonato. 'It is most wonderful that she should so dote on Benedick, whom she in all outward behaviour seemed ever to dislike.' Claudio confirmed all this with saying, that Hero had told him Beatrice was so in love with Benedick that she would certainly die of grief if he could not be brought to love her. This Leonato and Claudio seemed to agree was impossible, he having always been such a railer against all fair ladies, and in particular against Beatrice.

The prince affected to hearken to all this with great compassion for Beatrice, and he said, 'It were good that Benedick were told of this.'

'To what end?' said Claudio; 'he would but make sport of it, and torment the poor lady worse.'

'And if he should,' said the prince, 'it were a good deed to hang him, for Beatrice is an excellent sweet lady, and exceeding wise in everything but in loving Benedick.' Then the prince motioned to his companions that they should walk on, and leave Benedick to meditate upon what he had overheard.

Benedick had been listening with great eagerness to this conversation, and he said to himself when he heard Beatrice loved him, 'Is it possible? Sits the wind in that corner?'

When they were gone he began to reason in this manner with himself. 'This can be no trick! they were very serious, and they have the truth from Hero, and seem to pity the lady. Love me! Why, it must be requited! I did never think to marry. But when I said I should die a bachelor I did not think I should live to be married. They say the lady is virtuous and fair. She is so. And wise in everything but in loving me. Why, that is no great argument of her folly. But here comes Beatrice. By this day, she is a fair lady. I do spy some marks of love in her.'

Beatrice now approached him, and said with her usual tartness, 'Against my will I am sent to bid you come in to dinner.' Benedick, who never felt himself disposed to speak so politely to her before, replied, 'Fair Beatrice, I thank you for your pains.'

When Beatrice, after two or three more rude speeches, left him, Benedick thought he observed a concealed meaning of kindness under the uncivil words she uttered, and he said aloud, 'If I do not take pity on her, I am a villain. If I do not love her, I am a Jew. I will go get her picture.'

* * *

The gentleman being thus caught in the net they had spread for him, it was now Hero's turn to play her part with Beatrice. For this purpose she sent for Ursula and Margaret, two gentlewomen who attended upon her, and she said to Margaret, 'Good Margaret, run to the parlour; there you will find my cousin Beatrice talking with the prince and Claudio. Whisper in her ear that Ursula and I are walking in the orchard, and that our discourse is all of her. Bid her steal into that pleasant arbour, where honeysuckles, ripened by the sun, like ungrateful minions, forbid the sun to enter.'

This arbour into which Hero desired Margaret to entice Beatrice was the very same pleasant arbour where Benedick had so lately been an attentive listener. 'I will make her come, I warrant presently,' said Margaret.

Hero then, taking Ursula with her into the orchard, said to her, 'Now, Ursula, when Beatrice comes we will walk up and down this alley, and our talk must be only of Benedick, and when I name him let it be your part to praise him more than ever man did merit. My talk to you must be how Benedick is in love with Beatrice. Now begin, for look where Beatrice, like a lapwing, runs close by the ground, to hear our conference.'

They then began, Hero saying, as if in answer to something which Ursula had said, 'No, truly, Ursula, she is too disdainful, her spirits are as coy as wild birds of the rock.'

'But are you sure,' said Ursula, 'that Benedick loves Beatrice so entirely?'

Hero replied, 'So says the prince and my Lord Claudio, and they entreated me to acquaint her with it, but I persuaded them, if they loved Benedick, never to let Beatrice know of it.'

'Certainly,' replied Ursula, 'it were not good she knew his love, lest she made sport of it.'

'Why to say truth,' said Hero, 'I never yet saw a man, how wise soever, or noble, young or rarely featured, but she would dispraise him.'

'Sure, sure, such carping is not commendable,' said Ursula.

'No,' replied Hero, 'but who dare tell her so? If I should speak, she would mock me into air.'

'O you wrong your cousin,' said Ursula; 'she cannot be so much without true judgment as to refuse so rare a gentleman as Signor Benedick.'

'He hath an excellent good name,' said Hero;

'indeed he is the first man in Italy, always excepting my dear Claudio.'

Now, Hero giving her attendant a hint that it was time to change the discourse, Ursula said, 'And when are you to be married, madam?'

Hero then told her that she was to be married to Claudio the next day, and desired she would go in with her and look at some new attire, as she wished to consult with her on what she would wear on the morrow.

Beatrice, who had been listening with breath-

less eagerness to this dialogue, when they went away, exclaimed, 'What fire is in my ears? Can this be true? Farewell, contempt and scorn, and maiden pride, adieu! Benedick, love on; I will requite you, taming my wild heart to your loving hand.'

It must have been a pleasant sight to see these old enemies converted into new and loving friends, and to behold their first meeting after being cheated into mutual liking by the merry artifice of the good-humoured prince. But a sad reverse in the fortunes of Hero must now be thought of. The morrow, which was to have been her wedding day, brought sorrow on the heart of Hero and her good father Leonato.

The prince had a half-brother, who came from the wars along with him to Messina. This brother (his name was Don John) was a sad, discontented man, whose spirits seemed to labour in the contriving of villainies. He hated the prince his brother, and he hated Claudio because he was the prince's friend, and determined to prevent Claudio's marriage with Hero only for the wicked pleasure of making Claudio and the prince unhappy; for he knew the prince had set his heart upon this marriage almost as much as Claudio himself, and to effect this wicked purpose he employed one Borachio, a man as bad as himself, whom he encouraged with the offer of a great reward.

This Borachio paid his court to Margaret, Hero's attendant; and Don John knowing this, prevailed upon him to make Margaret promise to talk with him from her lady's chamber window that night, after Hero was asleep, and also to dress herself in Hero's clothes, the better to deceive Claudio into the belief that it was Hero, for that was the end he meant to compass by this wicked plot.

Don John then went to the prince and Claudio, and told them that Hero was an imprudent lady, and that she talked with men from her chamber window at midnight. Now this was the evening before the wedding, and he offered to take them that night where they should themselves hear Hero discoursing with a man from her window.

They consented to go along with him, and Claudio said, 'If I see anything tonight why I should not marry her, tomorrow in the church, where I intended to wed her, there will I shame her.'

The prince also said, 'And as I assisted you to obtain her, I will join with you to disgrace her.'

When Don John brought them near Hero's chamber that night, they saw Borachio standing under the window, and they saw Margaret looking out of Hero's window, and heard her talking with Borachio. Margaret being dressed in the same clothes they had seen Hero wear, the prince and Claudio believed it was the Lady Hero herself.

Nothing could equal the anger of Claudio when he had made, as he thought, this discovery. All his love for the innocent Hero was at once converted into hatred, and he resolved to expose her in the church, as he had said he would, the next day. The prince agreed to this, thinking that no punishment could be too severe for the naughty lady who talked with a man from her window the very night before she was going to be married to the noble Claudio.

*   *   *

The next day they were all met to celebrate the marriage, and Claudio and Hero were standing before the priest, and the priest, or friar, as he was called, was proceeding to pronounce the marriage ceremony, when Claudio, in the most passionate language, proclaimed the guilt of the blameless Hero, who, amazed at the strange words he uttered, said meekly:

'Is my lord well that he does speak so wide?'

Leonato, in the utmost horror, said to the prince:

'My lord, why speak not you?'

'What should I speak?' said the prince; 'I stand dishonoured, that have gone about to link my dear friend to an unworthy woman. Leonato, upon my honour, myself, my brother, and this grieved Claudio did see and hear her last night at midnight talk with a man at her chamber window.'

Benedick, in astonishment at what he had heard, said, 'This looks not like a marriage.'

'True, O God!' replied the heart-struck Hero; and then this hapless lady sank down in a fainting fit to all appearance dead. The prince and Claudio left the church without staying to see if Hero would recover, or at all regarding the distress into which they had thrown Leonato. So hard-hearted had their anger made them.

Benedick remained, and assisted Beatrice to recover Hero from her swoon, saying, 'How does the lady?'

'Dead, I think,' replied Beatrice in great agony, for she loved her cousin. Knowing her virtuous principles, she believed nothing of what she had heard spoken against her. Not so the poor old father; he believed the story of his child's fault, and it was piteous to hear him lamenting over her as she lay like one dead before him, wishing she might never more open her eyes.

But the ancient friar was a wise man and full of observation on human nature, and he had attentively marked the lady's countenance when she heard herself accused, and noted a thousand blushing shames to start into her face, and then he saw an angel-like whiteness bear away those blushes, and in her eye he saw a fire that did belie the error that the prince did speak against her maiden truth, and he said to the sorrowing father, 'Call me a fool; trust not my reading, or my observation; trust not my age, my reverence, or my calling, if this sweet lady lie not guiltless here under some biting error.'

When Hero recovered from the swoon into which she had fallen, the friar said to her, 'Lady, what man is he you are accused of?'

Hero replied, 'They know that do accuse me; I know of none.' Then turning to Leonato she said, 'O my father, if you can prove that any man has ever conversed with me at hours unmeet, or that I yesternight exchanged words with any creature, refuse me, hate me, torture me to death.'

'There is,' said the friar, 'some strange mis-understanding in the prince and Claudio.' Then he counselled Leonato that he should report that Hero was dead. He said that the death-like swoon in which they had left Hero would make this easy of belief; and he also advised him that he should put on mourning, and erect a monument for her, and do all rites that appertain to a burial.

'What will this do?'

The friar replied, 'This report of her death shall change slander into pity; that is some good, but that is not all the good I hope for. When Claudio shall hear she died upon hearing his words, the idea of her life shall sweetly creep into his imagination. Then shall he mourn, if ever love had interest in his heart, and wish he had not so accused her; yea, though he thought his accusation true.'

Benedick now said, 'Leonato, let the friar advise you; and though you know how well I love the prince and Claudio, yet on my honour I will not reveal this secret to them.'

Leonato, thus persuaded, yielded, and he said sorrowfully, 'I am so grieved that the smallest twine may lead me.' The kind friar then led Leonato and Hero away to comfort and console them, and Beatrice and Benedick remained alone. This was the meeting from which their friends, who contrived the merry plot against them, expected so much diversion. Those friends who were now overwhelmed with affliction, and from whose minds all thoughts of merriment seemed for ever banished.

Benedick was the first who spoke, and said, 'Lady Beatrice, have you wept all this while?'

'Yea, and I will weep a while longer,' said Beatrice.

'Surely,' said Benedick, 'I do believe your fair cousin is wronged.'

'Ah!' said Beatrice, 'how much might that man deserve of me who would right her!'

Benedick then said, 'Is there any way to show such friendship? I do love nothing in the world so well as you; is not that strange?'

'It were as possible,' said Beatrice, 'for me to say I loved nothing in this world so well as you; but believe me not, and yet I lie not. I confess nothing, and I deny nothing. I am sorry for my cousin.'

'By my sword,' said Benedick, 'you love me, and I protest I love you. Come, bid me do anything for you.'

'Kill Claudio,' said Beatrice.

'Ha! not for the wide world,' said Benedick; for he loved his friend Claudio, and he believed he had been imposed upon.

'Is not Claudio a villain, that has slandered, scorned, and dishonoured my cousin?' said Beatrice. 'O that I were a man!'

'Hear me, Beatrice!' said Benedick.

But Beatrice would hear nothing in Claudio's

defence, and she continued to urge on Benedick to revenge her cousin's wrongs. She said, 'Talk with a man out of the window; a proper saying. Sweet Hero! she is wronged; she is slandered; she is undone. O that I were a man for Claudio's sake, or that I had any friend who would be a man for my sake! but valour is melted into courtesies and compliments. I cannot be a man with wishing, therefore I will die a woman with grieving.'

'Tarry, good Beatrice,' said Benedick; 'by this hand I love you.'

'Use it for my love some other way than swearing by it,' said Beatrice.

'Think you, on your soul, that Claudio has wronged Hero?' asked Benedick.

'Yea,' answered Beatrice, 'as sure as I have a thought, or a soul.'

'Enough,' said Benedick; 'I am engaged; I will challenge him. I will kiss your hand, and so leave you. By this hand Claudio shall render me a dear account! As you hear from me, so think of me. Go, comfort your cousin.'

*   *   *

While Beatrice was thus powerfully pleading with Benedick, and working his gallant temper, by the spirit of her angry words, to engage in the cause of Hero, and fight even with his dear friend Claudio, Leonato was challenging the prince and Claudio to answer with their swords the injury they had done his child, who, he affirmed, had died for grief. But they respected his age and his sorrow, and they said, 'Nay, do not quarrel with us, good old man.'

Now came Benedick, and he also challenged Claudio to answer with his sword the injury he had done to Hero; and Claudio and the prince said to each other, 'Beatrice has set him on to do this.' Claudio nevertheless must have accepted this challenge of Benedick had not the justice of Heaven at the moment brought to pass a better proof of the innocence of Hero than the uncertain fortune of a duel.

While the prince and Claudio were yet talking of the challenge of Benedick, a magistrate brought Borachio as a prisoner before the prince. Borachio had been overheard talking with one of his companions of the mischief he had been employed by Don John to do.

Borachio made a full confession to the prince, in Claudio's hearing, that it was Margaret dressed in her lady's clothes that he had talked with from the window, whom they had mistaken for the Lady Hero herself, and no doubt continued on the minds of Claudio and the prince of the innocence of Hero. If a suspicion had remained it must have been removed by the flight of Don John, who, finding his villainies were detected, fled from Messina to avoid the just anger of his brother.

The heart of Claudio was sorely grieved when he found he had falsely accused Hero, who, he thought, died upon hearing his cruel words; and the memory of his beloved Hero's image came over him, in the rare semblance that he loved it first; and the prince asking him if what he heard did not run like iron through his soul, he answered, that he felt as if he had taken poison while Borachio was speaking.

The repentant Claudio implored forgiveness of the old man Leonato for the injury he had done his child, and promised that whatever penance Leonato would lay upon him for his fault in believing the false accusation against his betrothed wife, for her dear sake he would endure it.

The penance Leonato enjoined him was to marry the next morning a cousin of Hero's, who, he said, was now his heir, and in person very like Hero. Claudio, regarding the solemn promise he had made to Leonato, said he would marry this lady, even though she were an Ethiop; but his heart was very sorrowful, and he passed that night in tears, and in remorseful grief, at the tomb which Leonato had erected for Hero.

When the morning came, the prince accompanied Claudio to the church, where the good friar, and Leonato and his niece, were already assembled to celebrate a second wedding. Leonato presented to Claudio his promised bride, and she wore a mask, that Claudio might not discover her face. Claudio said to the lady in the mask, 'Give me your hand before this holy friar; I am your husband, if you will marry me.'

'And when I lived I was your other wife,' said this unknown lady, and, taking off her mask, she proved to be no niece (as was pretended), but Leonato's very daughter, the Lady Hero herself. We may be sure that this proved a most agreeable surprise to Claudio, who thought her dead, so that he could scarcely for joy believe his eyes. The prince, who was equally amazed at what he saw, exclaimed, 'Is not this Hero, Hero that was dead?'

Leonato replied, 'She died, my lord, but while her slander lived.'

The friar promised them an explanation of this seeming miracle after the ceremony was ended, and was proceeding to marry them, when he was interrupted by Benedick, who desired to be married at the same time to Beatrice. Beatrice making some demur to this match, and Benedick challenging her with her love for him, which he had learned from Hero, a pleasant explanation took place. They found they had both been tricked into a belief of love which had never existed, and had become lovers in truth by the power of a false jest. But the affection, which a merry invention had cheated them into, was grown too powerful to be shaken by a serious explanation, and since Benedick proposed to marry, he was resolved to think nothing to the purpose that the world could say against it. He merrily kept up the jest, and swore to Beatrice that he took her but for pity, and because he heard that she was dying of love for him. Beatrice protested that she yielded but upon great persuasion, and partly to save his life, for she heard he was in a consumption.

So these two mad wits were reconciled, and made a match of it, after Claudio and Hero were married, To complete the history, Don John, the contriver of the villainy, was taken in his flight and brought back to Messina, and a brave punishment it was to this gloomy and discontented man to see the joy and feastings which, by the disappointment of his plots, took place in the palace in Messina.

3

A Midsummer-Night's Dream

THERE WAS A LAW in the city of Athens which gave to its citizens the power of compelling their daughters to marry whomsoever they pleased. For upon a daughter's refusing to marry the man her father had chosen to be her husband, the father was empowered by this law to cause her to be put to death. But, as fathers do not often desire the death of their own daughters, even though they do happen to prove a little difficult to deal with, this law was seldom or never put in execution though perhaps the young ladies of that city were not infrequently threatened by their parents with the terrors of it.

There was one instance, however, of an old man, whose name was Egeus, who actually did come before Theseus (at that time the reigning duke of Athens) to complain that his daughter Hermia, whom he had commanded to marry Demetrius, a young man of a noble Athenian family, refused to obey him, because she loved another young Athenian, named Lysander. Egeus demanded justice of Theseus, and desired that this cruel law might be put in force against his daughter.

Hermia pleaded in excuse for her disobedience that Demetrius had formerly professed love for her dear friend Helena, and that Helena loved Demetrius. But this honourable reason which Hermia gave for not obeying her father's command moved not the stern Egeus.

Theseus, though a great and merciful prince, had no power to alter the laws of his country. Therefore he could only give Hermia four days to consider it, and at the end of that time, if she still refused to marry Demetrius, she was to be put to death.

When Hermia was dismissed from the presence of the duke she went to her lover Lysander, and told him of the peril she was in, and that she must either give up him and marry Demetrius or lose her life in four days.

Lysander was in great sorrow at hearing these evil tidings. But recollecting that he had an aunt who lived at some distance from Athens, and that at the place where she lived the cruel law could not be put in force against Hermia (this law not extending beyond the boundaries of the city), he proposed to Hermia that she should steal out of her father's house that night and go with him to his aunt's house, where he would marry her.

'I will meet you,' said Lysander, 'in the wood a few miles without the city, in that delightful wood where we have so often walked with Helena in the pleasant month of May.'

To this proposal Hermia joyfully agreed, and she told no one of her intended flight but her friend Helena. Helena (as maidens will do foolish things for love) resolved to go and tell this to Demetrius, though she could hope no benefit from betraying her friend's secret but the poor pleasure of following her faithless lover to the wood; for she well knew that Demetrius would go thither in pursuit of Hermia.

The wood in which Lysander and Hermia proposed to meet was the favourite haunt of those little beings known by the name of *Fairies*.

Oberon the king, and Titania the queen, of the Fairies, with all their tiny train of followers, in this wood held their midnight revels.

Between this little king and queen of sprites there happened at this time a sad quarrel. They never met in moonlight in the shady walks of this pleasant wood but they were quarrelling, till all their fairy elves would creep into acorn-cups and hide themselves for fear.

The cause of this unhappy disagreement was

Titania's refusing to give Oberon a little change-ling boy, whose mother had been Titania's friend, and upon her death the fairy queen stole the child from his nurse, and brought him up in the woods.

The night on which the lovers were to meet in this wood, as Titania was walking with some of her maids of honour she met Oberon, attended by his train of fairy courtiers.

'Ill met by moonlight, proud Titania,' said the fairy king.

The queen replied, 'What, jealous Oberon, is it you? Fairies, skip hence; I have forsworn his company.'

'Tarry, rash fairy,' said Oberon; 'am not I thy lord? Why does Titania cross her Oberon? Give me your little changeling boy to be my page.'

'Set your heart at rest,' answered the queen; 'your whole fairy kingdom buys not the boy of me.' She then left her lord in great anger.

'Well, go your way,' said Oberon; 'before the morning dawns I will torment you for this injury.'

Oberon then sent for Puck, his chief favourite and privy councillor.

Puck (or, as he was sometimes called, Robin Goodfellow) was a shrewd and knavish sprite, and used to play comical pranks in the neighbouring villages, sometimes getting into the dairies and skimming the milk, sometimes plunging his light and airy form into the butter-churn, and while he was dancing his fantastic shape in the churn, in vain the dairymaid would labour to change her cream into butter. Nor had the village swains any better success. Whenever Puck chose to play his freaks in the brewing copper the ale was sure to be spoiled. When a few good neighbours were met to drink some comfortable ale together, Puck would jump into the bowl of ale in the likeness of a roasted crab, and when some old goody was going to drink he would bob against her lips, and spill the ale over her withered chin; and presently after, when the same old dame was gravely seating herself to tell her neighbours a sad story, Puck would slip her three-legged stool from under her, and down toppled the poor old woman, and then the old gossips would hold their sides and laugh at her, and vow they never wasted a merrier hour.

'Come hither, Puck,' said Oberon to this little merry wanderer of the night; 'bring me the flower which maids call *Love in Idleness*; the juice of that little purple flower laid on the eyelids of those who sleep will make them, when they awake, dote on the first thing they see. Some of the juice of that flower I will drop on the eyelids of my

Titania when she is asleep, and the first thing she looks upon when she opens her eyes she will fall in love with, even though it be a lion, or a bear, a meddling monkey, or a busy ape. Before I will take this charm from off her sight, which I can do with another charm I know of, I will make her give me that boy to be my page.'

*　　*　　*

Puck who loved mischief to his heart, was highly diverted with this intended frolic of his master, and ran to seek the flower. While Oberon was waiting the return of Puck, he observed Demetrius and Helena enter the wood. He overheard Demetrius reproaching Helena for following him, and after many unkind words on his part, and gentle expostulations from Helena, reminding him of his former love and professions of true faith to her, he left her, as he said, to the mercy of the wild beasts, and she ran after him as swiftly as she could.

The fairy king, who was always friendly to true lovers, felt great pity for Helena. Perhaps, as Lysander said they used to walk by moonlight in this pleasant wood, Oberon might have seen Helena in those happy times when she was beloved by Demetrius.

However that might be, when Puck returned with the little purple flower, Oberon said to his favourite, 'Take a part of this flower; there has been a sweet Athenian lady here, who is in love with a disdainful youth; if you find him sleeping, drop some of the love-juice in his eyes, but contrive to do it when she is near him, that the first thing he sees when he awakes may be this despised lady. You will know the man by the Athenian garments which he wears.'

Puck promised to manage this matter very cleverly. Then Oberon went, unperceived by Titania, to her bower, where she was preparing to go to rest. Her fairy bower was a bank where grew wild thyme, cowslips, and sweet violets under a canopy of woodbine, musk-roses, and eglantine. There Titania always slept some part of the night; her coverlet the enamelled skin of a snake, which, though a small mantle, was wide enough to wrap a fairy in.

He found Titania giving orders to her fairies how they were to employ themselves while she slept.

'Some of you,' said her majesty, 'must kill cankers in the musk-rose buds, and some wage war with the bats for their leathern wings, to make for my small elves coats; and some of you keep watch that the clamorous owl that nightly hoots come not near me; but first sing me to sleep.' Then they began to sing this song:

> You spotted snakes with double tongue,
> Thorny hedgehogs be not seen;
> Newts and blind-worms do no wrong,
> Come not near our Fairy Queen.
> Philomel, with melody,
> Sing in your sweet lullaby,
> Lulla, lulla, lullaby; lulla, lulla, lullaby;
> Never harm, nor spell, nor charm,
> Come our lovely lady nigh;
> So good night with lullaby.

When the fairies had sung their queen asleep with this pretty lullaby, they left her to perform the important services she had enjoined them. Oberon then softly drew near his Titania, and dropped some of the love-juice on her eyelids, saying:

> What thou seest, when thou dost wake,
> Do it for thy true love take.

But to return to Hermia, who made her escape out of her father's house that night, to avoid the death she was doomed to for refusing to marry Demetrius. When she entered the wood she found her dear Lysander waiting for her to conduct her to his aunt's house. But before they had passed half through the wood, Hermia was so tired that, Lysander, who was very careful of this dear lady, who had proved her affection for him even by hazarding her life for his sake, persuaded her to rest till morning on a bank of soft moss, and lying down himself on the ground at some little distance, they soon fell fast asleep.

Here they were found by Puck, who, seeing a handsome young man asleep, and perceiving that his clothes were made in the Athenian fashion, and that a pretty lady was sleeping near him, concluded that this must be the Athenian maid and her disdainful lover whom Oberon had sent him to seek. He naturally enough thought that, as they were alone together, she must be the first thing he would see when he awoke. So, without more ado, he proceeded to pour some of the juice of the little purple flower into his eyes. But it so fell out that Helena came that way, and, instead of Hermia, she was the first object Lysander beheld when he opened his eyes. Strange to relate, so powerful was the love-charm, all his love for Hermia vanished away, and Lysander fell in love with Helena.

Had he first seen Hermia when he awoke, the blunder Puck committed would have been of no consequence, for he could not love that faithful lady too well. But for poor Lysander to be forced by a fairy love-charm to forget his own true Hermia, and to run after another lady, and leave

Hermia asleep quite alone in a wood at midnight, was a sad chance indeed.

Thus this misfortune happened. Helena, as has been before related, endeavoured to keep pace with Demetrius when he ran away so rudely from her. But she could not continue this unequal race long, men being always better runners in a long race than ladies. Helena soon lost sight of Demetrius. As she was wandering about, dejected and forlorn, she arrived at the place where Lysander was sleeping.

'Ah!' said she, 'this is Lysander lying on the ground: is he dead or asleep?' Then gently touching him, she said, 'Good sir, if you are alive, awake.'

Upon this Lysander opened his eyes, and, the love-charm beginning to work, immediately addressed her in terms of love and admiration, telling her she as much excelled Hermia in beauty as a dove does a raven, and that he would run through fire for her sweet sake, and many more such lover-like speeches. Helena, knowing Lysander was her friend Hermia's lover, and that he was solemnly engaged to marry her, was in the utmost rage when she heard herself addressed in this manner. For she thought, as well she might, that Lysander was making a jest of her.

'Oh!' said she, 'why was I born to be mocked

and scorned by everyone? Is it not enough, is it not enough, young man, that I can never get a sweet look or a kind word from Demetrius, but you, sir, must pretend in this disdainful manner to court me? I thought, Lysander, you were a lord of more true gentleness.' Saying these words in great anger, she ran away; and Lysander followed her, quite forgetful of his own Hermia, who was still asleep.

*   *   *

When Hermia awoke, she was in a sad fright at finding herself alone. She wandered about the wood, not knowing what was become of Lysander, or which way to go to seek for him. In the meantime Demetrius, not being able to find Hermia and his rival Lysander, and worn-out with his fruitless search, was observed by Oberon fast asleep.

Oberon had learnt, by some questions he had asked of Puck, that he had applied the love-charm to the wrong person's eyes. Now, having found the person first intended, he touched the eyelids of the sleeping Demetrius with the love-juice, and he instantly awoke. The first thing he saw being Helena, he, as Lysander had done before, began to address love-speeches to her. Just at that moment Lysander, followed by Hermia (for through Puck's unlucky mistake it was now Hermia's turn to run after her lover), made his appearance. Then Lysander and Demetrius, both speaking together, made love to Helena, they being each one under the influence of the same potent charm.

The astonished Helena thought that Demetrius, Lysander, and her once dear friend Hermia, were all in a plot together to make a jest of her.

Hermia was as much surprised as Helena. She knew not why Lysander and Demetrius, who both before loved her, were now become the lovers of Helena, and to Hermia the matter seemed to be no jest.

The ladies, who before had always been the dearest of friends, now fell to high words together.

'Unkind Hermia,' said Helena, 'it is you who have set Lysander on to vex me with mock praises and your other lover Demetrius, who used almost to spurn me with his foot, have you not bid him call me goddess, nymph, rare, and precious? He would not speak thus to me, whom he hates, if you did not set him on to make a jest of me. Unkind Hermia, to join with men in scorning your poor friend. Have you forgotten our school-day friendship? How often, Hermia, have we two, sitting on one cushion, both singing one song, with our needles working on the same flower, both on the same sampler wrought; growing up together in fashion of a double cherry, scarcely seeming parted? Hermia, it is not friendly in you, it is not maidenly, to join with men in scorning your poor friend.'

'I am amazed at your words,' said Hermia. 'I scorn you not; it seems you scorn me.'

'Ay, do,' returned Helena; 'persevere, feign serious looks, and make mouths at me when I turn my back; then wink at each other, and hold the sweet jest up. If you had any pity, grace, or manners you would not use me thus.'

While Helena and Hermia were speaking these angry words to each other, Demetrius and Lysander left them to fight together in the wood for the love of Helena.

When they found the gentlemen had left them, they departed and once more wandered weary in the wood in search of their lovers.

As soon as they were gone the fairy king, who, with little Puck, had been listening to their quarrels, said to him, 'This is your carelessness, Puck; or did you do this wilfully?'

'Believe me, king of shadows,' answered Puck, 'it was a mistake; did not you tell me I should know the man by his Athenian garments?

However, I am not sorry this has happened, for I think their jangling makes me excellent sport.'

'You heard,' said Oberon, 'that Demetrius and Lysander are gone to seek a convenient place to fight in. I command you to overhang the night with a thick fog, and lead these quarrelsome lovers so astray in the dark that they shall not be able to find each other. Counterfeit each of their voices to the other, and with bitter taunts provoke them to follow you, while they think it is their rival's tongue they hear. See you do this till they are so weary that they can go no farther, and when you find they are asleep drop the juice of this other flower into Lysander's eyes, and when he awakes he will forget his new love for Helena, and return to his old passion for Hermia, and then the two fair ladies may each one be happy with the man she loves, and they will think all that has passed a dream. About this quickly, Puck, and I will go and see what sweet love my Titania has found.'

Titania was still sleeping, and Oberon, seeing a clown near her who had lost his way in the wood, and was likewise asleep; 'This fellow,' said he, 'shall be my Titania's true love,' and, clapping an ass's head over the clown's, it seemed to fit him as well as if it had grown upon his own shoulders. Though Oberon fixed the ass's head on very

gently, it awakened him, and rising up unconscious of what Oberon had done to him, he went
towards the bower where the fairy queen slept.
All who saw him fled, till he came to the queen.

'Ah! what angel is that I see?' said Titania,
opening her eyes, and the juice of the little purple
flower beginning to take effect: 'Are you as wise
as you are beautiful?'

'Why, mistress,' said the clown, 'if I have wit
enough to find my way out of this wood, I have
enough to serve my turn.'

'Out of the wood do not desire to go,' said the
enamoured queen. 'I am a spirit of no common
rate. I love you. Go with me and I will give you
fairies to attend upon you.'

She then called four of her fairies. Their names
were Pease-blossom, Cobweb, Moth, and Mustard-
seed.

'Attend,' said the queen, 'upon this sweet
gentleman: hop in his walks and gambol in his
sight. Feed him with grapes and apricots, and
steal for him the honey-bags from the bees.'

'Come, sit with me,' said she to the clown, 'and
let me play with your amiable hairy cheeks, my
beautiful ass! and kiss your fair large ears, my
gentle joy!'

'Where is Pease-blossom?' said the ass-headed
clown, not much regarding the fairy queen's

courtship, but very proud of his new attendants.

'Here, sir,' said little Pease-blossom.

'Scratch my head,' said the clown. 'Where is Cobweb?'

'Here, sir,' said Cobweb.

'Good Mr. Cobweb,' said the foolish clown, 'kill me the red humble bee on the top of that thistle yonder; and, good Mr. Cobweb, bring me the honey-bag. Do not fret yourself too much in the action, Mr. Cobweb, and take care the honey-bag break not; I should be sorry to have you over-flown with a honey-bag. Where is Mustard-seed?'

'Here, sir,' said Mustard-seed; 'what is your will?'

'Nothing,' said the clown, 'good Mr. Mustard-seed, but to help Mr. Pease-blossom to scratch. I must go to a barber's, Mr. Mustard-seed, for methinks I am marvellous hairy about the face.'

'My sweet love,' said the queen, 'what will you have to eat? I have a venturous fairy who shall seek the squirrel's hoard and bring you some new nuts.'

'I had rather have a handful of dried peas,' said the clown, who with his ass's head had got an ass's appetite. 'But, I pray, let none of your people disturb me, for I have a mind to sleep.'

'Sleep then,' said the queen, 'and I will wind you in my arms. O how I love you! How I dote upon you!'

When the fairy king saw the clown sleeping in the arms of his queen, he advanced within her sight, and reproached her with having lavished her favours upon an ass.

This she could not deny, as the clown was then sleeping within her arms, with his ass's head crowned by her with flowers.

When Oberon had teased her for some time, he again demanded the changeling-boy, which she, ashamed of being discovered by her lord with her new favourite, did not dare to refuse him.

Oberon, having thus obtained the little boy he had so long wished for to be his page, took pity on the absurd situation into which, by his merry plan, he had brought his Titania, and threw some of the juice of the other flower into her eyes. The fairy queen immediately recovered her senses, and wondered at her late dotage, saying how she now loathed the sight of the strange monster.

Oberon likewise took the ass's head from off the clown, and left him to finish his nap with his own fool's head upon his shoulders.

Oberon and his Titania being now perfectly reconciled, he related to her the history of the lovers, and their midnight quarrels. She agreed to go with him and see the end of their adventures.

*   *   *

The fairy king and queen found the lovers and their fair ladies at no great distance from each other, sleeping on a grass plot; for Puck, to make amends for his former mistake, had contrived, with the utmost diligence, to bring them all to the same spot, unknown to each other; and he had carefully removed the charm from off the eyes of Lysander with the antidote the fairy king gave to him.

Hermia first awoke, and finding her lost Lysander asleep so near her, was looking at him and wondering at his strange inconstancy. Lysander presently opening his eyes, and seeing his Hermia, recovered his reason which the fairy charm had before clouded, and with his reason, his love for Hermia. They began to talk over the adventures of the night, doubting if these things had really happened, or if they had both been dreaming the same bewildering dream.

Helena and Demetrius were by this time awake; and a sweet sleep having quieted Helena's disturbed and angry spirits, she listened with delight to the professions of love which Demetrius still made to her, and which, to her surprise as well as pleasure, she began to perceive were sincere.

These fair night-wandering ladies, now no longer rivals, became once more true friends. All the unkind words which had passed were forgiven, and they calmly consulted together what was best to be done in their present situation. It was soon agreed that, as Demetrius had given up his pretensions to Hermia, he should endeavour to prevail upon her father to revoke the cruel sentence of death which had been passed against her. Demetrius was preparing to return to Athens for this friendly purpose when they were surprised with the sight of Egeus, Hermia's father, who came to the wood in pursuit of his runaway daughter.

When Egeus understood that Demetrius would not now marry his daughter, he no longer opposed her marriage with Lysander, but gave his consent that they should be wedded on the fourth day from that time, being the same day on which Hermia had been condemned to lose her life. On that same day Helena joyfully agreed to marry her beloved and now faithful Demetrius.

The fairy king and queen, who were unseen spectators of this reconciliation, and now saw the happy ending of the lovers' history brought about through the good offices of Oberon, received so much pleasure, that these kind spirits resolved to celebrate the approaching marriages with sports and revels throughout their kingdom.

And now, if any are offended with this story of fairies and their pranks, as judging it very difficult to believe and strange, they have only to think that they have been asleep and dreaming, and that all these adventures were visions which they saw in their sleep. I hope none of my readers will be so unreasonable as to be offended with a pretty, harmless Midsummer Night's Dream.

4

The Winter's Tale

LEONTES, KING OF SICILY, and his queen, the beautiful and virtuous Hermione, once lived in the greatest harmony together. So happy was Leontes in the love of this excellent lady, that he had no wish ungratified, except that he sometimes desired to see again, and to present to his queen, his old companion and schoolfellow, Polixenes, King of Bohemia. Leontes and Polixenes were brought up together from their infancy, but being by the death of their fathers called to reign over their respective kingdoms, they had not met for many years, though they frequently interchanged gifts, letters, and loving embassies.

At length, after repeated invitations, Polixenes came from Bohemia to the Sicilian court, to make his friend Leontes a visit.

At first this visit gave nothing but pleasure to Leontes. He recommended the friend of his youth to the queen's particular attention, and seemed, in the presence of his dear friend and old companion, to have his happiness quite completed. They talked over old times; their school-days and their youthful pranks were remembered, and recounted to Hermione, who always took a cheerful part in these conversations.

When, after a long stay, Polixenes was preparing to depart, Hermione, at the desire of her husband, joined her entreaties to his that Polixenes would prolong his visit.

And now began this good queen's sorrow; for Polixenes, refusing to stay at the request of Leontes, was won over by Hermione's gentle and persuasive words to put off his departure for some weeks longer. Upon this, although Leontes had so long known the honourable principles of his friend Polixenes, as well as the excellent disposition of his virtuous queen, he was seized with an ungovernable jealousy. Every attention Hermione showed Polixenes, though by her husband's particular desire, and merely to please him, increased the unfortunate king's jealousy, and from being a loving and true friend, and the best and fondest of husbands, Leontes became suddenly a savage and inhuman monster. Sending for Camillo, one of the lords of his court, and telling him of the suspicion he entertained, he commanded him to poison Polixenes.

Camillo was a good man; and he, well knowing

that the jealousy of Leontes had not the slightest foundation in truth, instead of poisoning Polixenes, acquainted him with the king his master's orders, and agreed to escape with him out of the Sicilian dominions. Polixenes, with the assistance of Camillo, arrived safe in his own kingdom of Bohemia, where Camillo lived from that time in the king's court, and became the chief friend and favourite of Polixenes.

The flight of Polixenes enraged the jealous Leontes still more. He went to the queen's apartment, where the good lady was sitting with her little son Mamillus, who was just beginning to tell one of his best stories to amuse his mother, when the king entered, and, taking the child away, sent Hermione to prison.

Mamillus, though but a very young child, loved his mother tenderly. When he saw her so dishonoured, and found she was taken from him to be put into a prison, he took it deeply to heart, and drooped and pined away by slow degrees, losing his appetite and his sleep, till it was thought his grief would kill him.

The king, when he had sent his queen to prison, commanded Cleomenes and Dion, two Sicilian lords, to go to Delphos, there to enquire of the oracle at the temple of Apollo if his queen had been unfaithful to him.

When Hermione had been a short time in prison, she was presented with a daughter. The poor lady received much comfort from the sight of her pretty baby, and she said to it, 'My poor little prisoner, I am as innocent as you are.'

Hermione had a kind friend in the noble-spirited Paulina, who was the wife of Antigonus, a Sicilian lord; and when the Lady Paulina heard her royal mistress was ill, she went to the prison where Hermione was confined. She said to Emilia, a lady who attended upon Hermione, 'I pray you, Emilia, tell the good queen, if her majesty dare trust me with her little babe, I will carry it to the king its father. We do not know how he may soften at the sight of his innocent child.'

'Most worthy madam,' replied Emilia, 'I will acquaint the queen with your noble offer. She was wishing today that she had any friend who would venture to present the child to the king.'

'And tell her,' said Paulina, 'that I will speak boldly to Leontes in her defence.'

'May you be for ever blessed,' said Emilia, 'for your kindness to our gracious queen!' Emilia then went to Hermione, who joyfully gave up her baby to the care of Paulina, for she had feared that no one would dare venture to present the child to its father.

*   *   *

Paulina took the new-born infant, and forcing herself into the king's presence, notwithstanding her husband, fearing the king's anger, endeavoured to prevent her, she laid the babe at its father's feet, and Paulina made a noble speech to the king in defence of Hermione, and she reproached him severely for his inhumanity, and implored him to have mercy on his innocent wife and child. But Paulina's spirited remonstrances only increased Leontes' displeasure, and he ordered her husband Antigonus to take her from his presence.

When Paulina went away, she left the little baby at its father's feet, thinking, when he was alone with it, he would look upon it, and have pity upon its helpless innocence.

The good Paulina was mistaken. For no sooner was she gone than the merciless father ordered Antigonus, Paulina's husband, to take the child, and carry it out to sea, and leave it upon some desert shore to perish.

Antigonus, unlike the good Camillo, too well obeyed the orders of Leontes. He immediately carried the child on shipboard, and put out to sea, intending to leave it on the first desert coast he could find.

So firmly was the king persuaded of the guilt of Hermione, that he would not wait for the return of Cleomenes and Dion, whom he had sent to consult the oracle of Apollo at Delphos. Before the queen was recovered from her illness, and from the grief for the loss of her precious baby, he had her brought to a public trial before all the lords and nobles of his court. And when all the great lords, the judges, and all the nobility of the land were assembled together to try Hermione, and that unhappy queen was standing as a prisoner before her subjects to receive their judgment, Cleomenes and Dion entered the assembly, and presented to the king the answer of the oracle sealed up. Leontes commanded the seal to be broken, and the words of the oracle to be read aloud. These were the words: 'Hermione is innocent, Polixenes blameless, Camillo a true subject, Leontes a jealous tyrant, and the king shall live without an heir if that which is lost be not found.'

The king would give no credit to the words of the oracle. He said it was a falsehood invented by the queen's friends, and he desired the judge to proceed in the trial of the queen. But while Leontes was speaking a man entered and told him that the Prince Mamillus, hearing his mother was to be tried for her life, struck with grief and shame had suddenly died.

Hermione, upon hearing of the death of this

dear affectionate child, who had lost his life in sorrowing for her misfortune, fainted, and Leontes, pierced to the heart by the news, began to feel pity for his unhappy queen, and he ordered Paulina, and the ladies who were her attendants, to take her away, and use means for her recovery. Paulina soon returned, and told the king that Hermione was dead.

When Leontes heard that the queen was dead, he repented of his cruelty to her. Now that he thought his ill usage had broken Hermione's heart, he believed her innocent; and he now thought the words of the oracle were true, as he knew 'if that which was lost was not found', which he concluded was his young daughter, he should be without an heir, the young Prince Mamillus being dead. He would give his kingdom now to recover his lost daughter; and Leontes gave himself up to remorse, and passed many years in mournful thoughts and repentant grief.

The ship in which Antigonus carried the infant princess out to sea was driven by a storm upon the coast of Bohemia, the very kingdom of the good King Polixenes. Here Antigonus landed, and here he left the little baby.

*   *   *

Antigonus never returned to Sicily to tell Leontes where he had left his daughter, for as he was going back to the ship, a bear came out of the woods, and tore him to pieces, a just punishment on him for obeying the wicked order of Leontes.

The child was dressed in rich clothes and jewels for Hermione had made it very fine when she sent it to Leontes, and Antigonus had pinned a paper to its mantle, with the name of *Perdita* written thereon, and words obscurely intimating its high birth and untoward fate.

This poor deserted baby was found by a shepherd. He was a humane man, and so he carried the little Perdita home to his wife, who nursed it tenderly. But poverty tempted the shepherd to conceal the rich prize he had found; therefore he left that part of the country, that no one might know where he got his riches, and with part of Perdita's jewels he bought herds of sheep, and became a wealthy shepherd. He brought up Perdita as his own child, and she knew not she was any other than a shepherd's daughter.

The little Perdita grew up a lovely maiden; and though she had no better education than that of a shepherd's daughter, yet so did the natural graces she inherited from her royal mother shine forth in her untutored mind that no one from her behaviour would have known she had not been brought up in her father's court.

Polixenes, the King of Bohemia, had an only son, whose name was Florizel. As this young prince was hunting near the shepherd's dwelling he saw the old man's supposed daughter, and the beauty, modesty, and queenlike bearing of Perdita caused him instantly to fall in love with her. He soon, under the name of Doricles, and in the disguise of a private gentleman, became a constant visitor at the old shepherd's house.

Florizel's frequent absence from court alarmed Polixenes, and, setting people to watch his son, he discovered his love for the shepherd's fair daughter.

Polixenes then called for Camillo, the faithful Camillo, who had preserved his life from the fury of Leontes, and desired that he would accompany him to the house of the shepherd, the supposed father of Perdita.

Polixenes and Camillo, both in disguise, arrived at the old shepherd's dwelling while they were celebrating the feast of sheep-shearing, and though they were strangers, yet at the sheep-shearing, every guest being made welcome, they were invited to walk in and join in the general festivity.

Nothing but mirth and jollity was going forward.

Tables were spread, and great preparations were making for the rustic feast. Some lads and lasses were dancing on the green before the house, while others of the young men were buying ribands, gloves, and such toys of a pedlar at the door.

While this busy scene was going forward, Florizel and Perdita sat quietly in a retired corner, seemingly more pleased with the conversation of each other than desirous of engaging in the sports and silly amusements of those around them.

The king was so disguised that it was impossible his son could know him; he therefore advanced near enough to hear the conversation. The simple yet elegant manner in which Perdita conversed with his son did not a little surprise Polixenes. He said to Camillo, 'This is the prettiest low-born lass I ever saw; nothing she does or says but looks like something greater than herself, too noble for this place.'

Camillo replied, 'Indeed she is the very queen of curds and cream.'

'Pray, my good friend,' said the king to the old shepherd, 'what fair swain is that talking with your daughter?' 'They call him Doricles,' replied the shepherd. 'He says he loves my daughter, and to speak the truth there is not a kiss to choose

which loves the other best. If young Doricles can get her she shall bring him that he little dreams of,' meaning the remainder of Perdita's jewels, which, after he had bought herds of sheep with part of them, he had carefully hoarded up for her marriage portion.

Polixenes then addressed his son. 'How, now, young man!' said he; 'your heart seems full of something that takes off your mind from feasting. When I was young, I used to load my love with presents; but you have let the pedlar go, and bought your lass no toy.'

The young prince, who little thought he was talking to the king his father, replied, 'Old sir, she prizes not such trifles; the gifts which Perdita expects from me are locked up in my heart.'

Then, turning to Perdita, he said to her, 'Oh, hear me, Perdita, before this ancient gentleman, who, it seems, was once himself a lover; he shall hear what I profess.' Florizel then called upon the old stranger to be a witness to a solemn promise of marriage which he made to Perdita, saying to Polixenes, 'I pray you mark our contract.'

'Mark your divorce, young sir,' said the king, discovering himself. Polixenes then reproached his son for daring to contract himself to this low-born maiden, calling Perdita 'shepherd's brat, sheep-hook,' and other disrespectful names; and threatening, if ever she suffered his son to see her again, he would put her and the old shepherd her father to a cruel death.

The king then left them in great wrath, and ordered Camillo to follow him with Prince Florizel.

*   *   *

When the king had departed, Perdita, whose royal nature was roused by Polixenes' reproaches, said, 'Though we are all undone, I was not much afraid; and once or twice I was about to speak, and tell him plainly that the selfsame sun which shines upon his palace hides not his face from our cottage, but looks on both alike.' Then sorrowfully she said, 'But now I am awakened from this dream, I will queen it no further. Leave me, sir; I will go milk my ewes and weep.'

The kind-hearted Camillo was charmed with the spirit and propriety of Perdita's behaviour; and perceiving that the young prince was too deeply in love to give up his mistress at the command of his royal father, he thought of a way to befriend the lovers, and, at the same time, to execute a favourable scheme he had in his mind.

Camillo had long known that Leontes, the King of Sicily, was become a true penitent, and though Camillo was now the favoured friend of King Polixenes, he could not help wishing once more to see his late royal master and his native home. He therefore proposed to Florizel and Perdita that they should accompany him to the Sicilian court, where he would engage Leontes should protect them, till, through his mediation, they could obtain pardon from Polixenes, and his consent to their marriage.

To this proposal they joyfully agreed; and Camillo, who conducted everything relative to their flight, allowed the old shepherd to go along with them.

The shepherd took with him the remainder of Perdita's jewels, her baby clothes, and the paper which he had found pinned to her mantle.

After a prosperous voyage, Florizel and Perdita, Camillo and the old shepherd, arrived in safety at the court of Leontes. Leontes, who still mourned his dead Hermione and his lost child, received Camillo with great kindness, and gave a cordial welcome to Prince Florizel. But Perdita, whom Florizel introduced as his princess, seemed to engross all Leontes' attention. Perceiving a resemblance between her and his dead Queen Hermione, his grief broke out afresh, and he said, such a lovely creature might his own daughter have been if he had not so cruelly destroyed her. 'And then, too,' said he to Florizel, 'I lost the society and friendship of your brave father, whom I now desire more than my life once again to look upon.'

When the old shepherd heard how much notice the king had taken of Perdita, and that he had lost a daughter who was exposed in infancy, he fell to comparing the time when he found the little Perdita, with the manner of its exposure, the jewels and other tokens of its high birth, from all which it was impossible for him not to conclude that Perdita and the king's lost daughter were the same.

Florizel and Perdita, Camillo and the faithful Paulina were present when the old shepherd related to the king the manner in which he had found the child, and also the circumstance of Antigonus' death, he having seen the bear seize him. He showed the rich mantle in which Paulina remembered Hermione had wrapped the child, and he produced a jewel which she remembered Hermione had tied about Perdita's neck. He gave up the paper which Paulina knew to be the writing of her husband; it could not be doubted that Perdita was Leontes' own daughter; but oh, the noble struggles of Paulina between sorrow for her husband's death and joy that the oracle was fulfilled in the king's heir, his long-lost daughter, being found! When Leontes heard that Perdita was his daughter, the great sorrow that he felt that Hermione was not living to behold her child made him that he could say nothing for a long time, but 'O thy mother, thy mother!'

Paulina interrupted this joyful yet distressful scene, with saying to Leontes that she had a statue newly finished by that rare Italian master, Julio Romano, which was such a perfect resemblance of the queen, that would his majesty be pleased to go to her house and look upon it, he would almost be ready to think it was Hermione herself. Thither then they all went; the king anxious to see the semblance of his Hermione, and Perdita longing to behold what the mother she never saw did look like.

When Paulina drew back the curtain which concealed this famous statue, so perfectly did it resemble Hermione that all the king's sorrow was renewed at the sight; for a long time he had no power to speak or move.

'I like your silence, my liege,' said Paulina: 'it the more shows your wonder. Is not this statue very like your queen?'

At length the king said, 'O thus she stood, even with such majesty, when I first wooed her. But yet, Paulina, Hermione was not so aged as this statue looks.'

Paulina replied, 'So much the more the carver's

excellence, who has made the statue as Hermione would have looked had she been living now. But let me draw the curtain, sire, lest presently you think it moves.'

The king then said, 'Do not draw the curtain. Would I were dead. See, Camillo, would you not think it breathed? Her eye seems to have motion in it.'

'I must draw the curtain, my liege,' said Paulina. 'You are so transported you are persuaded the statue lives.'

'O sweet Paulina,' said Leontes, 'make me think so twenty years together. Still methinks there is an air comes from her. What fine chisel could ever yet cut breath? Let no man mock me, for I will kiss her.'

'Good, my lord, forbear!' said Paulina. 'The ruddiness upon her lips is wet; you will stain your own with oily painting. Shall I draw the curtain?'

'No, not these twenty years,' said Leontes.

Perdita, who all this time had been kneeling and beholding in silent admiration the statue of her matchless mother, said now, 'And so long could I stay here, looking upon my dead mother.'

'Either forbear this transport,' said Paulina to Leontes, 'and let me draw the curtain, or prepare yourself for more amazement. I can make the statue move indeed, aye, and descend from off the pedestal and take you by the hand. But then you will think (which I protest I am not) that I am assisted by some wicked powers.'

'What you can make her do,' said the astonished king, 'I am content to look upon. What you can make her speak I am content to hear; for it is as easy to make her speak as move.'

Paulina then ordered some slow and solemn music, which she had prepared for the purpose, to strike up, and to the amazement of all the beholders the statue came down from off the pedestal, and threw its arms around Leontes' neck. The statue then began to speak, praying for blessings on her husband, and on her child, the newly-found Perdita.

No wonder that the statue hung upon Leontes' neck, and blessed her husband and her child. No wonder; for the statue was indeed Hermione herself, the real and living queen.

Paulina had falsely reported to the king the death of Hermione, thinking that the only means to preserve her royal mistress's life. With the good Paulina, Hermione had lived ever since, never choosing Leontes should know she was living till she heard Perdita was found; for though she had long forgiven the injuries which Leontes had done to herself she could not pardon his cruelty to his infant daughter.

His dead queen thus restored to life, his lost daughter found, the long-sorrowing Leontes could scarcely support the excess of his own happiness.

Nothing but congratulations and affectionate speeches were heard on all sides. Now the delighted parents thanked Prince Florizel for loving their lowly-seeming daughter; and now they blessed the good old shepherd for preserving their child. Greatly did Camillo and Paulina rejoice that they had lived to see so good an end of all their faithful services.

And as if nothing should be wanting to complete this strange and unlooked-for joy, King Polixenes himself now entered the palace.

When Polixenes first missed his son and Camillo, knowing that Camillo had long wished to return to Sicily, he thought that he should find the fugitives here; and following them with all speed, he happened to arrive just at this the happiest moment of Leontes' life.

Polixenes took a part in the general joy. He forgave his friend Leontes the unjust jealousy he had conceived against him, and they once more loved each other with all the warmth of their first boyish friendship. And there was no fear that Polixenes would now oppose his son's marriage with Perdita. She was no 'sheep-hook' now, but the heiress of the crown of Sicily.

Thus have we seen the patient virtues of the long-suffering Hermione rewarded. That excellent lady lived many years with her Leontes and her Perdita, the happiest of mothers and of queens.

5

—◦❀⟶ ❀◉ ∴ ◉❀ ⟵❀ ◦—

The Merchant Of Venice

SHYLOCK, THE JEW, lived at Venice. He was a usurer, who had gathered together an immense fortune by lending money at great interest to Christian merchants. Shylock, being a hard-hearted man, exacted the payment of the money he lent with such severity that he was much disliked by all good men, and particularly by Antonio, a young merchant of Venice. Shylock hated Antonio just as much, because he used to lend money to people in distress, and would never take any interest for the money he lent. Therefore there was great enmity between this covetous Jew and the generous merchant Antonio. Whenever Antonio met Shylock on the Rialto (or Exchange) he used to reproach him with his usuries and hard dealings, which the Jew would bear with seeming patience, while he secretly planned revenge.

Antonio was the kindest man that lived, the best natured, and had the most unwearied spirit in doing good deeds. Indeed, he was one in whom the ancient Roman honour more appeared than in any that drew breath in Italy. He was greatly beloved by all his fellow citizens. But the friend who was the nearest and dearest to his heart was Bassanio, a noble Venetian, who, having but a small estate, had nearly spent all his little fortune by living at too high a rate for his slender means, as young men of high rank with small fortunes are too apt to do. Whenever Bassanio wanted money, Antonio assisted him, and it seemed as if they had but one heart and one purse between them.

One day Bassanio came to Antonio, and told him that he wished to repair his fortune by a wealthy marriage with a lady whom he dearly loved, whose father, but lately dead, had left her sole heiress to a large estate. He said that in her father's lifetime he used to visit at her house, when he thought he had observed this lady had sometimes from her eyes sent speechless messages that seemed to say he would be no unwelcome lover. But not having money to furnish himself with an appearance befitting the lover of so rich an heiress, he besought Antonio to add to the many favours he had shown him by lending him three thousand ducats.

Antonio had no money by him at that time to

lend his friend. But expecting soon to have some ships come home laden with merchandise, he said he would go to Shylock, the rich money-lender, and borrow the money upon the credit of those ships.

Antonio and Bassanio went together to Shylock, and Antonio asked the Jew to lend him three thousand ducats upon an interest he should require to be paid out of the merchandise contained in his ships at sea. On this Shylock thought within himself, 'If I can once catch him on the hip, I will feed fat the ancient grudge I bear him. He hates our Jewish nation; he lends out money gratis; and among the merchants he rails at me and my well-earned bargains, which he calls interest. Cursed be my tribe if I forgive him!' Antonio, finding he was musing within himself and did not answer, and being impatient for the money, said, 'Shylock, do you hear—will you lend the money?'

To this question the Jew replied: 'Signor Antonio, on the Rialto many a time and often you have railed at me about my monies and my usuries, and I have borne it with a patient shrug, for sufferance is the badge of all our tribe; and then you have called me unbeliever, cut-throat dog, and spit upon my Jewish garments, and spurned at me with your foot, as if I were a cur.

Well, then, it now appears you need my help; and you come to me and say, "*Shylock, lend me monies*". Has a dog money? Is it possible a cur should lend three thousand ducats? Shall I bend low and say, Fair sir, you spit upon me on Wednesday last, another time you called me dog, and for these courtesies I am to lend you money?'

Antonio replied: 'I am as like to call you so again, to spit on you again, and spurn you too. If you will lend me this money, lend it not to me as to a friend, but rather lend it me as to an enemy, that if I break you may with better face exact the penalty.'

'Why, look you,' said Shylock, 'how you storm! I would be friends with you and have your love. I will forget the shames you have put upon me. I will supply your wants and take no interest for my money.'

This seemingly kind offer greatly surprised Antonio. Then Shylock, still pretending kindness, and that all he did was to gain Antonio's love, again said he would lend him the three thousand ducats, and take no interest for his money; only Antonio should go with him to a lawyer and there sign in merry sport a bond that if he did not repay the money by a certain day he would forfeit a pound of flesh, to be cut off from any part of his body that Shylock pleased.

'Content,' said Antonio; 'I will sign to this bond, and say there is much kindness in the Jew.'

Bassanio said Antonio should not sign to such a bond for him. Still Antonio insisted that he would sign it, for that before the day of payment came his ships would return laden with many times the value of the money.

Shylock, hearing this conversation, exclaimed: 'O, Father Abraham, what suspicious people these Christians are! Their own hard dealings teach them to suspect the thoughts of others. I pray you tell me this, Bassanio: If he should break this day, what should I gain by the execution of the forfeiture? A pound of man's flesh, taken from a man, is not so estimable, nor profitable either, as the flesh of mutton or beef. I say, to buy his favour I offer this friendship. If he will take it, so; if not, adieu.'

At last, against the advice of Bassanio, who, notwithstanding all the Jew had said of his kind intentions, did not like his friend should run the risk of this shocking punishment for his sake, Antonio signed the bond, thinking it really was, as the Jew said, merely in sport.

* * *

The rich heiress that Bassanio wished to marry lived near Venice, at a place called Belmont. Her name was Portia, and in the graces of her person and her mind she was nothing inferior to that Portia of whom we read, who was Cato's daughter and the wife of Brutus.

Bassanio, being so kindly supplied with money by his friend Antonio, at the hazard of his life, set out for Belmont with a splendid train, and attended by a gentleman of the name of Gratiano.

Bassanio proving successful in his suit, Portia in a short time consented to accept of him for a husband.

Bassanio confessed to Portia that he had no fortune, and that his high birth and noble ancestry were all that he could boast of. She, who loved him for his worthy qualities, and had riches enough not to regard wealth in a husband, answered with a graceful modesty that she would wish herself a thousand times more fair, and ten thousand times more rich, to be more worthy of him. Then the accomplished Portia prettily dispraised herself, and said she was an unlessoned girl, unschooled, unpractised, yet not so old but that she could learn, and that she would commit her gentle spirit to be directed and governed by him in all things. And she said, 'Myself and what is mine to you and yours is now converted. But

yesterday, Bassanio, I was the lady of this fair
mansion, queen of myself, and mistress over these
servants; and now this house, these servants, and
myself are yours, my lord; I give them with this
ring,' presenting a ring to Bassanio.

Bassanio was so overpowered with gratitude
and wonder at the gracious manner in which the
rich and noble Portia accepted of a man of his
humble fortunes, that he could not express his
joy and reverence to the dear lady who so honoured him by anything but broken words of love
and thankfulness. Taking the ring, he vowed
never to part with it.

Gratiano and Nerissa, Portia's waiting-maid,
were in attendance upon their lord and lady when
Portia so gracefully promised to become the
obedient wife of Bassanio. Gratiano, wishing
Bassanio and the generous lady joy, desired permission to be married at the same time.

'With all my heart, Gratiano,' said Bassanio,
'if you can get a wife.'

Gratiano then said that he loved the Lady
Portia's fair waiting-gentlewoman, Nerissa, and
that she had promised to be his wife if her lady
married Bassanio. Portia asked Nerissa if this was
true. Nerissa replied, 'Madam, it is so, if you
approve of it.' Portia willingly consenting,
Bassanio pleasantly said, 'Then our wedding-feast

shall be much honoured by your marriage, Gratiano.'

The happiness of these lovers was sadly crossed at this moment by the entrance of a messenger who brought a letter from Antonio containing fearful tidings. When Bassanio read Antonio's letter Portia feared it was to tell him of the death of some dear friend, he looked so pale; and inquiring what was the news which had so distressed him he said, 'Oh, sweet Portia, here are a few of the unpleasantest words that ever blotted paper. Gentle lady, when I first imparted my love to you I freely told you all the wealth I had ran in my veins, but I should have told you that I had less than nothing, being in debt.'

Bassanio then told Portia what has been here related of his borrowing the money of Antonio, and of Antonio's procuring it of Shylock the Jew, and of the bond by which Antonio had engaged to forfeit a pound of flesh if it was not repaid by a certain day. Then Bassanio read Antonio's letter, the words of which were—'Sweet Bassanio, my ships are all lost, my bond to the Jew is forfeited, and since in paying it is impossible I should live, I could wish to see you at my death; notwithstanding, use your pleasure; if your love for me do not persuade you to come, let not my letter.'

'Oh, my dear love,' said Portia, 'do quickly the

business and be gone; you shall have gold to pay the money twenty times over, before this kind friend shall lose a hair by my Bassanio's fault, and as you are so dearly bought I will dearly love you.' Portia then said she would be married to Bassanio before he set out, to give him a legal right to her money. That same day they were married, and Gratiano was also married to Nerissa, and Bassanio and Gratiano, the instant they were married, set out in great haste for Venice, where Bassanio found Antonio in prison.

*   *   *

The day of payment being past, the cruel Jew would not accept of the money which Bassanio offered him, but insisted upon having a pound of Antonio's flesh. A day was appointed to try this shocking cause before the Duke of Venice, and Bassanio awaited in dreadful suspense the opening of the trial.

When Portia parted with her husband she spoke cheeringly to him and bade him bring his dear friend along with him when he returned. Yet she feared it would go hard with Antonio, and when she was left alone, she began to think and consider within herself if she could by any means help to save the life of her dear Bassanio's friend. And

notwithstanding, when she wished to honour her
Bassanio, she had said to him with such a meek
and wife-grace that she would submit in all things
to be governed by his superior wisdom, yet, being
now called forth into action by the peril of her
honoured husband's friend, she did nothing
doubt her own powers, and by the sole guidance
of her own true and perfect judgment, at once
resolved to go herself to Venice and speak in
Antonio's defence.

Portia had a relation who was counsellor in the
law. To this gentleman, whose name was Bellario,
she wrote, and stating the case to him desired his
opinion, and that with his advice he would also
send her the dress worn by a counsellor. When the
messenger returned he brought letters from
Bellario of advice how to proceed, and also
everything necessary for her equipment.

Portia dressed herself and her maid Nerissa in
men's apparel, and, putting on the robes of a
counsellor, she took Nerissa along with her as
her clerk. Setting out immediately, they arrived
at Venice on the very day of the trial. The cause
was just going to be heard before the duke and
senators of Venice in the senate-house, when
Portia entered this high court of justice and presented a letter from Bellario, in which that learned
counsellor wrote to the duke, saying he would

have come himself to plead for Antonio, but that
he was prevented by sickness, and he requested
that the learned young doctor Balthasar (so he
called Portia) might be permitted to plead in his
stead. This the duke granted, much wondering
at the youthful appearance of the stranger, who
was prettily disguised by her counsellor's robes
and her large wig.

And now began this important trial. Portia
looked around her, and she saw the merciless Jew.
She saw Bassanio, but he knew her not in her
disguise. He was standing beside Antonio in an
agony of distress and fear for his friend.

The importance of the difficult task Portia had
engaged in gave this tender lady courage, and
she boldly proceeded in the duty she had to
perform. First of all she addressed herself to
Shylock; and allowing that he had a right by the
Venetian law to have the forfeit expressed in the
bond, she spoke so sweetly of the noble quality
of mercy, as would have softened any heart but
the unfeeling Shylock's; saying, that it dropped
as the gentle rain from heaven upon the place
beneath; and how mercy was a double blessing,
it blessed him that gave, and him that received it;
and how it became monarchs better than their
crowns, being an attribute of God himself, and
that earthly power came nearest to God's, in

proportion as mercy tempered justice; and she bade Shylock remember that as we all pray for mercy, that same prayer should teach us to show mercy.

Shylock only answered her by desiring to have the penalty forfeited in the bond. 'Is he not able to pay the money?' asked Portia. Bassanio then offered the Jew the payment of the three thousand ducats as many times over as he should desire, which Shylock refusing, and still insisting on having a pound of Antonio's flesh, Bassanio begged the learned young counsellor would try to change the law a little to save Antonio's life. But Portia gravely answered that laws once established must never be altered. Shylock hearing Portia say that the law might not be altered, it seemed to him that she was pleading in his favour, and he said, 'A Daniel is come to judgment! O wise young judge, how I do honour you! How much older are you than your looks!'

Portia now desired Shylock to let her look at the bond, and when she had read it, she said, 'This bond is forfeited, and by this the Jew may lawfully claim a pound of flesh, to be by him cut off nearest Antonio's heart.' Then she said to Shylock, 'Be merciful; take the money, and bid me tear the bond.'

But no mercy would the cruel Shylock show;

and he said, 'By my soul, I swear there is no power in the tongue of man to alter me.' 'Why then, Antonio,' said Portia, 'you must prepare your bosom for the knife.' While Shylock was sharpening a long knife with great eagerness to cut off the pound of flesh, Portia said to Antonio, 'Have you anything to say?' Antonio with a calm resignation, replied that he had but little to say, for that he had prepared his mind for death. Then he said to Bassanio, 'Give me your hand, Bassanio! Fare you well! Grieve not that I am fallen into this misfortune for you. Commend me to your honourable wife, and tell her how I have loved you!' Bassanio, in the deepest affliction replied, 'Antonio, I am married to a wife who is as dear to me as life itself. But life itself, my wife, and all the world, are not esteemed with me above your life. I would lose all, I would sacrifice all to this fiend here, to deliver you.'

Portia hearing this, though the kind-hearted lady was not at all offended with her husband for expressing the love he owed to so true a friend as Antonio in these strong terms, yet could not help answering, 'Your wife would give you little thanks if she were present to hear you make this offer.' And then Gratiano, who loved to copy what his lord did, thought he must make a speech like Bassanio's, and he said, in Nerissa's hearing, who was writing in her clerk's dress by the side of Portia, 'I have a wife, whom I protest I love. I wish she were in heaven, if she could but entreat some power there to change the cruel temper of this currish Jew.' 'It is well you wish this behind her back, else you would have but an unquiet house,' said Nerissa.

Shylock now cried out impatiently, 'We trifle time. I pray pronounce the sentence.' And now all was awful expectation in the court, and every heart was full of grief for Antonio.

*   *   *

Portia asked if the scales were ready to weigh the flesh; and she said to the Jew, 'Shylock, you must have some surgeon by, lest he bleed to death.' Shylock, whose whole intention was that Antonio should bleed to death, said, 'It is not so named in the bond.' Portia replied, 'It is not so named in the bond, but what of that? It were good you did so much for charity.'

To this all the answer Shylock would make was, 'I cannot find it; it is not in the bond.' 'Then,' said Portia, 'a pound of Antonio's flesh is thine. The law allows it, and the court awards it. And you may cut this flesh from off his breast. The law allows it, and the court awards it.' Again

Shylock exclaimed, 'O wise and upright judge! A Daniel is come to judgment!' And then he sharpened his long knife again, and looking eagerly on Antonio, he said, 'Come, prepare!'

'Tarry a little, Jew,' said Portia; 'there is something else. This bond here gives you no drop of blood; the words expressly are, "a pound of flesh". If in the cutting of the pound of flesh you shed one drop of Christian blood, your land and goods are by the law to be confiscated to the State of Venice.' Now, as it was utterly impossible for Shylock to cut off the pound of flesh without shedding some of Antonio's blood, this wise discovery of Portia's, that it was flesh and not blood that was named in the bond, saved the life of Antonio. All admired the wonderful wisdom of the young counsellor who had so happily thought of this, and applause resounded from every part of the senate-house. Gratiano exclaimed, in the words which Shylock had used, 'O wise and upright judge! mark, Jew, a Daniel is come to judgment!'

Shylock, finding himself defeated in his cruel intention, said with a disappointed look that he would take the money. Bassanio, rejoiced beyond measure at Antonio's unexpected deliverance, cried out, 'Here is the money!' But Portia stopped him, saying, 'Softly, there is no haste; the Jew shall have nothing but the penalty. Therefore, prepare, Shylock, to cut off the flesh, but mind you shed no blood, and do not cut off more or less than just a pound; be it more or less by one poor scruple, nay, if the scale turn but by the weight of a single hair, you are condemned by the laws of Venice to die, and all your wealth is forfeited to the senate.' 'Give me my money, and let me go,' said Shylock. 'I have it ready,' said Bassanio; 'here it is.'

Shylock was going to take the money, when Portia again stopped him, saying, 'Tarry, Jew; I have yet another hold upon you. By the laws of Venice your wealth is forfeited to the State for having conspired against the life of one of its citizens, and your life lies at the mercy of the duke. Therefore down on your knees and ask him to pardon you.'

The duke then said to Shylock, 'That you may see the difference of our Christian spirit, I pardon you your life before you ask it. Half your wealth belongs to Antonio, the other half comes to the State.'

The generous Antonio then said that he would give up his share of Shylock's wealth if Shylock would sign a deed to make it over at his death to his daughter and her husband. For Antonio knew that the Jew had an only daughter, who had lately married against his consent to a young Christian, named Lorenzo, a friend of Antonio's, which had so offended Shylock that he had disinherited her.

The Jew agreed to this, and being thus disappointed in his revenge and despoiled of his riches, he said, 'I am ill. Let me go home. Send the deed after me and I will sign over half my riches to my daughter.' 'Get thee gone, then,' said the duke, 'and sign it. If you repent your cruelty and turn Christian the State will forgive you the fine of the other half of your riches.'

*   *   *

The duke now released Antonio and dismissed the court. He then highly praised the wisdom and cleverness of the young counsellor, and invited him home to dinner. Portia, who meant to return to Belmont before her husband, replied, 'I humbly thank your grace, but I must away directly.' The duke said he was sorry he had not leisure to stay and dine with him, and turning to Antonio he added, 'Reward this gentleman. For in my mind you are much indebted to him.'

The duke and his senators left the court. Then Bassanio said to Portia, 'Most worthy gentleman, I and my friend Antonio have by your wisdom been this day acquitted of grievous penalties, and

I beg you will accept of three thousand ducats due unto the Jew.' 'And we shall stand indebted to you over and above,' said Antonio, 'in love and service evermore.'

Portia could not be prevailed upon to accept the money, but upon Bassanio still pressing her to accept of some reward, she said, 'Give me your gloves. I will wear them for your sake.' Then Bassanio, taking off his gloves, she espied the ring which she had given him upon his finger. Now it was the ring the wily lady wanted to get from him to make a merry jest when she saw Bassanio again that made her ask him for his gloves, and she said when she saw the ring, 'And for your love, I will take this ring from you.

Bassanio was sadly distressed that the counsellor should ask him for the only thing he could not part with, and he replied in great confusion that he could not give him that ring because it was his wife's gift, and he had vowed never to part with it. But he said that he would give him the most valuable ring in Venice, and find it out by proclamation. On this Portia affected to be affronted, and left the court saying, 'You teach me, sir, how a beggar should be answered.'

'Dear Bassanio,' said Antonio, 'let him have the ring. Let my love and the great service he has done for me be valued against your wife's displeasure.' Bassanio, ashamed to appear so ungrateful, yielded, and sent Gratiano after Portia with the ring. Then the *clerk* Nerissa, who had also given Gratiano a ring, begged his ring, and Gratiano, not choosing to be outdone in generosity by his lord, gave it to her. And there was laughing among these ladies, to think, when they got home, how they would tax their husbands with giving away their rings, and swear that they had given them as presents to some woman.

Portia, when she returned, was in that happy temper of mind which never fails to attend the consciousness of having performed a good action. Her cheerful spirits enjoyed everything she saw. The moon never seemed to shine so bright before, and when that pleasant moon was hid behind a cloud, then a light which she saw from her house at Belmont as well pleased her charmed fancy, and she said to Nerissa: 'That light we see is burning in my hall; how far that little candle throws its beams, so shines a good deed in a naughty world;' and hearing the sound of music from her house, she said: 'Methinks that music sounds much sweeter than by day.'

And now Portia and Nerissa entered the house, and, dressing themselves in their own apparel, they awaited the arrival of their husbands, who soon followed them with Antonio. Bassanio, presenting his dear friend to the Lady Portia, the congratulations and welcomings of that lady were hardly over when they perceived Nerissa and her husband quarrelling in a corner of the room. 'A quarrel already?' said Portia. 'What is the matter?' Gratiano replied: 'Lady, it is about a paltry gilt ring that Nerissa gave me, with words upon it like the poetry on a cutler's knife: *Love me, and leave me not.*'

'What does the poetry or the value of the ring signify?' said Nerissa. 'You swore to me, when I gave it to you, that you would keep it till the hour of death. Now you say you gave it to the lawyer's clerk. I know you gave it to a woman.'

'By this hand,' replied Gratiano, 'I gave it to a youth, a kind of boy, a little scrubbed boy no higher than yourself. He was clerk to the young counsellor, that by his wise pleading saved Antonio's life. This prating boy begged it for a fee, and I could not for my life deny him.' Portia said: 'You were to blame, Gratiano, to part with your wife's first gift. I gave my lord Bassanio a ring, and I am sure he would not part with it for all the world.' Gratiano, in excuse for his fault, now said: 'My lord Bassanio gave his ring away to the counsellor, and then the boy, his clerk, that took some pains in writing, he begged my ring.'

Portia, hearing this, seemed very angry, and

reproached Bassanio for giving away her ring. She said Nerissa had taught her what to believe, and that she knew some woman had the ring. Bassanio was very unhappy to have so offended his dear lady, and he said with great earnestness: 'No, by my honour, no woman had it, but a civil doctor, who refused three thousand ducats of me, and begged the ring, which when I denied him he went displeased away. What could I do, sweet Portia? I was so beset with shame for my seeming ingratitude that I was forced to send the ring after him. Pardon me, good lady; had you been there I think you would have begged the ring of me to give the worthy doctor.'

'Ah!' said Antonio, 'I am the unhappy cause of these quarrels.'

Portia bid Antonio not to grieve at that, for that he was welcome notwithstanding. Then Antonio said, 'I once did lend my body for Bassanio's sake. But for him to whom your husband gave the ring I should have now been dead. I dare be bound again, my soul upon the forfeit, your lord will never more break his faith with you.' 'Then you shall be his surety,' said Portia; 'give him this ring and bid him keep it better than the other.'

When Bassanio looked at this ring he was strangely surprised to find it was the same he gave away. Then Portia told him how she was the young counsellor, and Nerissa was her clerk. Bassanio found, to his unspeakable wonder and delight, that it was by the noble courage and wisdom of his wife that Antonio's life was saved.

And Portia again welcomed Antonio, and gave him letters which by some chance had fallen into her hands, which contained an account of Antonio's ships, that were supposed lost, being safely arrived in the harbour. So these tragical beginnings of this rich merchant's story were all forgotten in the unexpected good fortune which ensued. There was leisure to laugh at the comical adventure of the rings, and the husbands that did not know their own wives; Gratiano merely vowing, in a sort of rhyming speech, that

> ————while he lived, he'd fear no other thing
> So sore, as keeping safe Nerissa's ring.